THE GUITARIST'S LICK BOOK
by
PETER VOGL

HOW TO USE THE

If you are using the book and DVD together, follow these suggestions.

Step 1
Watch a section of the DVD. Watch again until you understand the section completely.

Step 2
Once you understand the section, go to the book to practice the scales and licks over and over until you are comfortable with them.

Step 3
After practicing with the book, go back to the DVD and play along to make sure you are performing the material properly.

This course is designed to be worked through, stopping and practicing each section until you are thoroughly familiar with it. It will probably take the average student 3-6 months to work all the way through the book and DVD, so don't get in a hurry. Take your time and learn the material correctly.

Copyright 2004 by Watch & Learn, Inc./Peter Vogl Second Edition
ALL RIGHTS RESERVED. Any copying, arranging, or adapting of this work without the consent of the owner is an infringement of copyright.

INTRODUCTION

The *Guitarist's Lick Book* teaches you 60 guitar licks played by famous guitarists that will add power and excitement to your solos. All licks and scales are written in both standard music notation and tablature, resulting in the student being able to use other instruction books upon completion of this course. Guitarists will learn how to build licks from scales, play the same lick in different keys, and add variety to existing licks.

Each lick is played slow and fast and then with a full band on the accompanying CD. This makes the learning process fun and enjoyable and quickly helps each guitarist take his playing to the next level.

THE AUTHOR

Peter Vogl, the author of this book, has been a professional performer and teacher in the Atlanta area for over 20 years. He was raised in Michigan and went to college at the University of Georgia, where he majored in classical guitar performance. He also did post graduate work at James Madison University. Peter has set up and directed 6 different schools of music in the Atlanta area and currently works at Jan Smith Studios as a session player and guitar instructor. He has written several instructional courses including *Introduction to Blues Guitar* Book & DVD, *Introduction to Rock Guitar* Book & DVD, *The Guitarist's Tablature Book, The Guitarist's Chord Book, The Guitarist's Scale Book, The Guitarist's Lick DVD*, and the *Let's Jam! CD Series* (six different jam along CDs).

COMPANION DVD

The companion DVD, *The Guitarist's Lick DVD*, is also available. It shows the correct movement and positions of both the left and right hands which can only be seen on screen. In addition, it covers the material in the book utilizing the latest in video technology (split screen, on screen tablature, state of the art graphics, special effects, and animation) to add further emphasis and clarity. This DVD is available at your local store or send $14.95 plus $4.00 shipping and handling to:

Watch & Learn, Inc.
1882 Queens Way
Atlanta, GA 30341
800-416-7088

CD & DVD Chapter Markers

The CD & DVD markers are included in this book to show where each lesson is located on the companion CD or DVD. Use your remote control on the CD or DVD player to skip to the track you want. Also use the menu system on the DVD to locate each lick. CDs are limited to 99 chapter markers, so there are many more DVD markers (over 200).

TABLE OF CONTENTS

SECTION 1 - Tuning & Techniques

	Page	CD	DVD
Tuning The Guitar	1	2	3
Relative Tuning	2		
Tablature	3		
Hammer Ons, Pull Offs, Trills, & Tapping	4-5	4	4-5
Slides, Bends, & Vibrato	6-8		6-7
Soloing Using Licks	9-10	5-6	8-9

Section 2 - Blues Licks in A Minor

	Page	CD	DVD
A Minor Pentatonic Scales	12	7	2.2-2.3
A Blues Scales	13		2.4-2.5
A Melodic Minor	13		2.6
Lick 1	14	8	2.7-2.8
Lick 2	14	9	2.9-2.10
Lick 3	14	10	2.11-2.12
Lick 4	15	11	2.13-2.14
Lick 5	15	12	2.15-2.16
Lick 6	15	13	2.17-2.18
Lick 7	16	14	2.19-2.20
Lick 8	16	15	2.21-2.22
Lick 9	16	16	2.23-2.24
Lick 10	17	17	2.25-2.26
Lick 11 + Chorus	17	18	2.27-2.28
Lick 12	18	19	2.29-2.30
Lick 13	18	20	2.31-2.32
Lick 14	18	21	2.33-2.34
Lick 15	19	22	2.35-2.36
Playing with Let's Jam! CDs	19-21	23	2.37-2.42

Section 3 - Rock Licks in G Minor

	Page	CD	DVD
G Minor Pentatonic Scales	23-24	24	3.1-3.4
G Blues Scale - 1st Position	24		3.5
G Dorian - 1st Position	24		3.6
Lick 1	25	25	3.7-3.8
Lick 2	25	26	3.9-3.10
Lick 3	25	27	3.11-3.12
Lick 4	26	28	3.13
Lick 5 + Flanger	26	29	3.14-3.17
Lick 6	26	30	3.18-3.19
Lick 7	27	31	3.20-3.21
Lick 8	27	32	3.22
Lick 9	27	33	3.23-3.24
Lick 10 + Wah	28	34	3.25-3.28
Lick 11	28	35	3.29-3.30
Lick 12	28	36	3.31
Lick 13	29	37	3.32-3.33
Lick 14	29	38	3.34-3.35
Lick 15 + Octaver	29	39	3.36-3.39
Playing with Let's Jam! CD	30-31	40	3.40-3.45

Section 4 - Blues Licks in A

	Page	CD	DVD
A Blues with Maj 3rd	33	41	4.1-4.2
A Minor Pentatonic Scales	33		4.3-4.4
A Major Pentatonic Scales	34		4.5-4.6
A Mixolydian	34		4.7
Lick 1	35	42	4.8-4.9
Lick 2	35	43	4.10-4.11
Lick 3	35	44	4.12-4.13

	Page	CD	DVD
Lick 4	36	45	4.14-4.15
Lick 5	36	46	4.16-4.17
Lick 6	36	47	4.18-4.19
Lick 7	37	48	4.20-4.21
Lick 8	37	49	4.22-4.23
Lick 9	37	50	4.24-4.25
Lick 10	38	51	4.26-4.27
Lick 11	38	52	4.28-4.29
Lick 12	38	53	4.30-4.31
Lick 13 + Harmonist	39	54	4.32-4.35
Lick 14	39	55	4.36
Lick 15	39	56	4.37-4.38
Playing with Let's Jam! CDs	40-41	57	4.39-4.44

Section 5 - Rock Lick in E

	Page	CD	DVD
E Blues	43	58	5.1-5.2
E Minor Pentatonic - 12th Fret	43		5.3
E Major Pentatonic	43-44		5.4
E Mixolydian	44		5.7
Lick 1	45	59	5.8-5.9
Lick 2	45	60	5.10-5.11
Lick 3	45	61	5.12-5.13
Lick 4	46	62	5.14-5.15
Lick 5	46	63	5.16-5.17
Lick 6	46	64	5.20
Lick 7	47	65	5.21-5.22
Lick 8	47	66	5.23-5.24
Lick 9	47	67	5.25-5.26
Lick 10	48	68	5.27-5.28
Lick 11	48	69	5.29-5.30
Lick 12	48	70	5.31-5.32
Lick 13	49	71	5.33-5.34
Lick 14 + Chorus	49	72	5.35-5.38
Lick 15 + Flanger	50	73	5.39-5.42
Playing with Let's Jam! CD	51-53	74	5.43-5.48

Section 6 - Playing in Other Keys

	Page	CD	DVD
Lick 2 in Am	55	75	6.1-6.2
Lick 2 in G Minor	55	76-77	6.3-6.5
Lick 2 In E Minor	56	78-79	6.6-6.7
Lick 1 in A	57	80	6.8
Lick 1 in E	57	81-82	6.9-6.10
Lick 1 in G	58	83-84	6.11-6.13
Lick 13 in E	59	85	6.14
Lick 13 in A	59	86-87	6.15-6.17
Lick 13 in G	60	88-89	6.18-6.21

Section 7 - Practicing with Let's Jam! CDs

	Page	CD	DVD
Exercise 1 & 2	62	90	6.22-6.25
Exercise 3 & 4	63		6.26-6.29
Practicing Licks with Let's Jam! CDs	64-65		6.30
Solo 1	67-68	91	
Solo 2	69	92	

Appendix - Arpeggios

	Page	CD	DVD
Arpeggios in A Minor	71		
Arpeggios in G Minor	72		
Arpeggios in A	73		
Arpeggios in E	74		
Let's Jam! CD - 4 Tracks		93-96	Special Features

SECTION 1
TUNING & TECHNIQUES

TUNING THE GUITAR

Before playing the guitar, it must be tuned to standard pitch. If you have a piano at home, it can be used as a tuning source. The following picture shows which note on the piano to tune each open string of the guitar to.

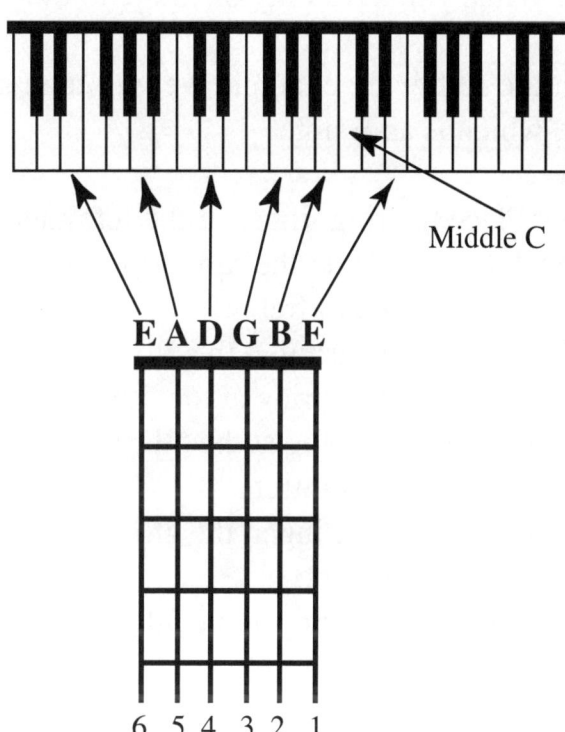

Note: If your piano hasn't been tuned recently, the guitar may not agree perfectly with a pitch pipe or tuning fork. Some older pianos are tuned a half step below standard pitch. In this case, use one of the following methods to tune.

DVD OR CD

It is recommended that you tune your guitar to the DVD or CD that accompanies this book so that you will be in tune when you play along with the songs and exercises.

ELECTRONIC TUNER

An electronic tuner is the fastest and most accurate way to tune a guitar. I highly recommend getting one. They are available for $20 - $50.

1

RELATIVE TUNING

Relative tuning means to tune the guitar to itself and is used in the following situations:

1. When you do not have an electronic tuner or other source to tune from.
2. When you have only one note to tune from.

In the following example we will tune all of the strings to the 6th string of the guitar, which is an E note.

1. Place the ring finger of the left hand behind the fifth fret of the 6th string to fret the 1st note. Tune the 5th string open (not fretted) until it sounds like the 6th string fretted at the 5th fret.
2. Fret the 5th string at the 5th fret. Tune the 4th string open (not fretted) until it sounds like the 5th string at the 5th fret.
3. Fret the 4th string at the 5th fret. Tune the 3rd string open until it sounds like the 4th string at the 5th fret.
4. Fret the 3rd string at the 4th fret. Tune the 2nd string until it sounds like the 3rd string at the 4th fret.
5. Fret the 2nd string at the 5th fret. Tune the 1st string open until it sounds like the 2nd string at the 5th fret.

Now repeat the above procedure to fine tune the guitar. Until your ear develops, have your teacher or a guitar playing friend check the tuning to make sure it is correct.

The following diagram of the guitar fret board illustrates the above procedure.

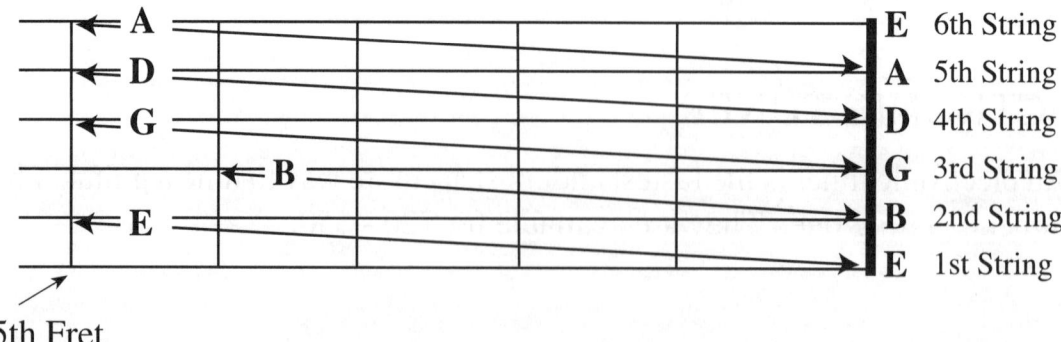

5th Fret

Note - Old dull strings lose their tonal qualities and sometimes tune incorrectly. Check with your teacher or favorite music store to make sure your strings are in good playing condition.

TABLATURE

This book is written in both tablature and standard music notation. If you wish to learn to read music, consult your local music store for a good book or ask your music teacher for an explanation. We will explain tablature because it is easy to learn if you are teaching yourself and because a lot of popular guitar music is available in tablature.

Tablature is a system for writing music that shows the proper string and fret to play and which fingers to use. In guitar tablature, each line represents a string on the guitar. If the string is to be fretted, the fret number is written on the appropriate line. Otherwise a 0 is written. Study the examples below until you understand them thoroughly.

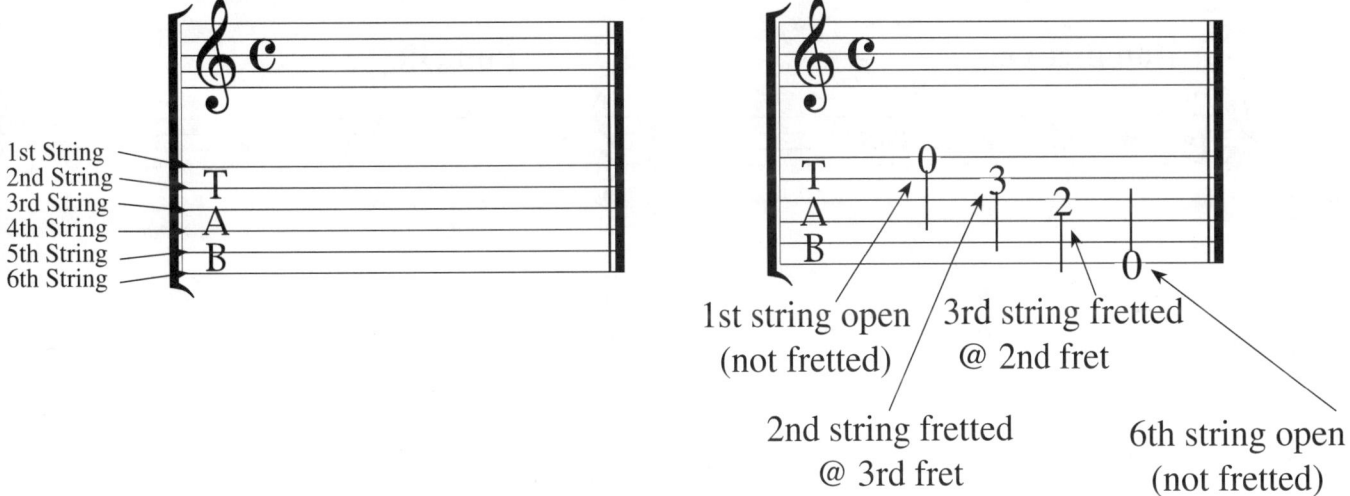

The music will be divided into either two sets of lines (staffs) or three sets of lines.

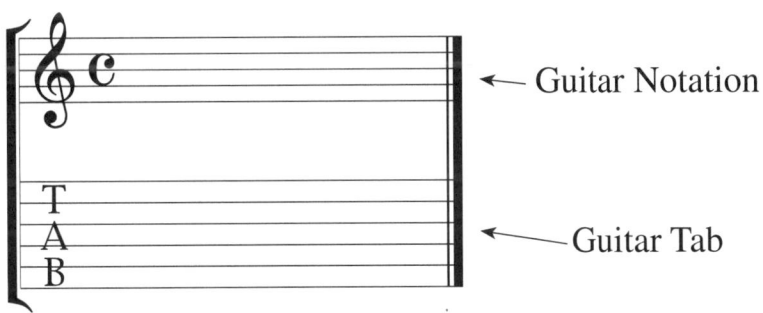

TECHNIQUES

Here are some fundamental techniques that are required for this book. If you are having difficulty with these techniques, try the *Intro To Rock Guitar* or *Intro To Blues Guitar* Book and DVD. They both clearly explain and demonstrate these techniques.

HAMMER ONS AND PULL OFFS

When playing a hammer on, pick the first note, then hammer on with a finger on your left hand. You will need to be on the tip of the finger and strike the note with velocity and accuracy.

When playing a pull off, again pick the first note, then pull off with a finger on your left hand. You will need to be on the tip of the finger. The finger you are pulling off to needs to hold the string stable during the pull off.

DOUBLE HAMMER ONS AND PULL OFFS

A double hammer on is executed by picking the first note and hammering on the next two notes. When pulling off, you should feel as if you're plucking the string with your finger. Both techniques require you to be on the tip of your fingers.

HAMMER ON PULL OFF COMBINATION

This technique starts by picking the first note, hammering on, and then pulling off back to the first note.

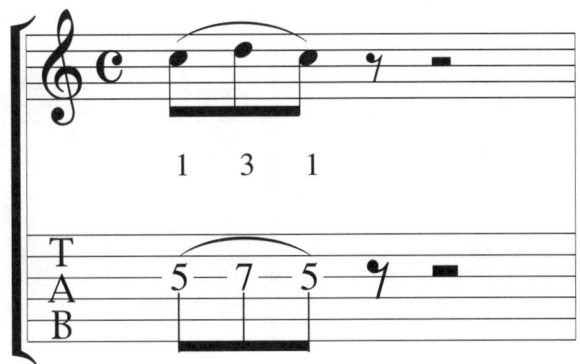

TRILLS

A trill is a repeated hammer on and pull off. Be sure to be on the tips of your fingers.

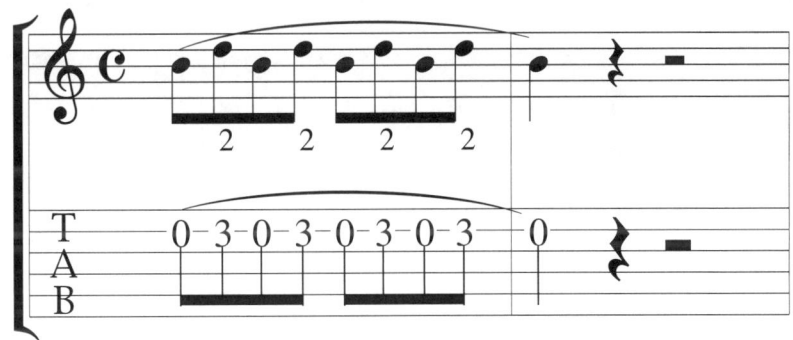

TAPPING

A tap is a hammer on and possibly a pull off with a finger on the right hand. By the way, there are some musicians who will argue the use of the term tap and what it should mean. Mostly, however, this is what tapping refers to.

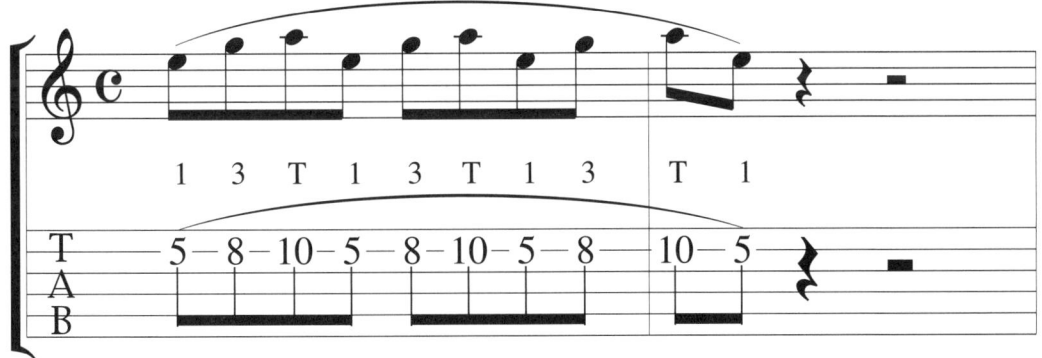

SLIDES

A slide means you pick a note and slide into another. Slides can move up or down and can be phrased many different ways.

SLIDES FROM A UNDETERMINED NOTE

This slide usually starts a fret or two away but sometimes further. It does not stay at the starting point long enough for the listener to really tell where it starts.

DOUBLE STOP SLIDES

This is a slide involving two notes. It is important that both fingers move evenly across the frets.

BENDS

When playing a bend, use all the fingers that are available to help execute the bend. With a third finger, for example, use the third finger to bend the note, the second finger on the same string helping to bend the note, and the first finger to mute the string above it. Compare the sound of your bends, hammer ons, and vibratos with the CD to make sure they sound the same. If you need to watch these techniques, they are available on the companion DVD.

BEND WITH A STATIONARY NOTE

Use your pinky to hold the note stationary on the first string and use the third and second finger to bend the second string a whole step. You can play them both at the same time or one after the other.

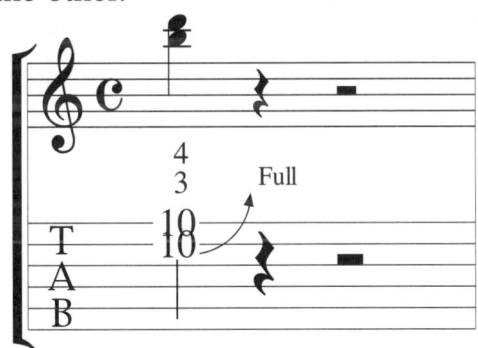

BEND WITH A HAMMER ON

This is a very legato sound. Hammer on to the seventh fret and then bend the note a whole step. You only pick the first note.

VIBRATO

A vibrato is a technique mostly used on the notes that are held or sustained for a while, like a last note of a phrase. It is a rhythmic moving of the string. Vibratos can be many speeds, from fast to slow.

If you need to see these techniques, try *The Guitarist's Lick DVD*.

THE EFFECTS OPTION

You will occasionally see this logo, caption, and an explanation. This is to give you ideas for using effects on the preceding lick such as a Wah Pedal or a Chorus. These effects are not necessary to play the lick but will add variety to your soloing. Check with your local music store to see what effects pedals are available.

SOLOING USING LICKS

When soloing, most guitarists use a combination of scales, arpeggios, and licks. How much of each is decided by each player. You should try to hide or bury the lick within a line. This means to play a lick within a melodic line you are creating. It may be in the middle of a scale idea or following or preceding an arpeggio. What we don't want is to play a lick, then immediately play another lick and another lick. You will be repeating yourself very quickly using this method. Try to be creative with your licks. Here is an example of hiding a lick within a line. Here is the lick.

Now here is the same lick buried within a line. The A minor pentatonic scale is used before and after this lick.

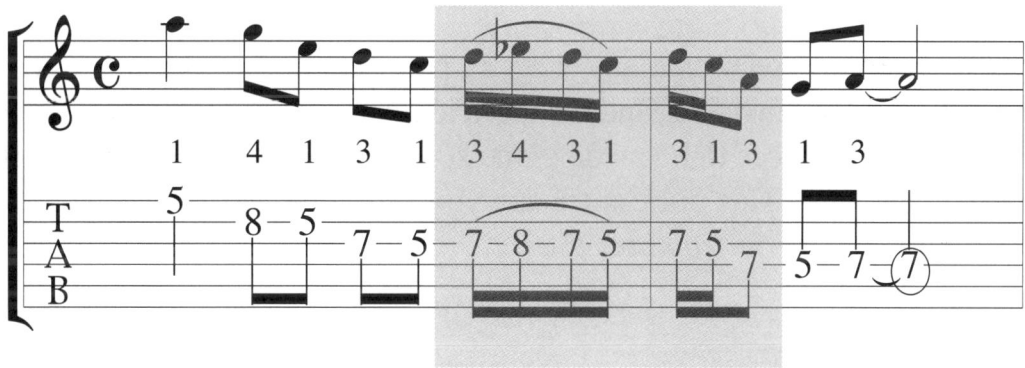

So this is the idea. Learn a lick, but also try to hide the lick. It isn't necessary to do this each and every time but it's a great technique to know and use.

LICKS & PHRASING

After learning to play a lick as written, another valuable step is to practice phrasing the same lick many different ways. This will enable you to make the lick your own and to possibly come up with a completely new lick based on your new phrasing. Phrasing refers to the manner in which you play music. It generally refers to rhythm, tempo, accents, and dynamics. In this case, it means to change the rhythm or try a different accent pattern. Try changing the speed or feel of the lick. Try the lick against different songs or jam tracks. Go as far as changing the order of notes or repeating one or subtracting a note or two.

Here is an example lick. Listen to the audio CD to hear how I phrase this lick several different ways.

Try this technique with as many licks as possible. Learn the lick, then try to change it. Make it your own idea and make it a logical, musical one. There is no right or wrong way, just choices to be made. One song or track might inspire a different phrasing than another. This does not mean you shouldn't learn the lick as written. Try learning the rule before you break it.

SECTION 2
BLUES LICKS IN A MINOR

The Licks in this section will all be in the key of A minor. To hear what these licks sound like, we will be using Track 4 of the *Let's Jam! CD Blues & Rock,* which is Track 93 on the companion CD. It is not necessary to have the *Let's Jam! CD* to learn these licks, but it will prove useful as you try to use them in different keys and chord progressions. There are several scales that will be used in this section. Below are the scales and positions you will need. Become comfortable with these before going on to the licks. For more scales and scale positions, try *The Guitarist's Scale Book.*

A MINOR PENTATONIC - 1ST POSITION

A MINOR PENTATONIC - 2ND POSITION

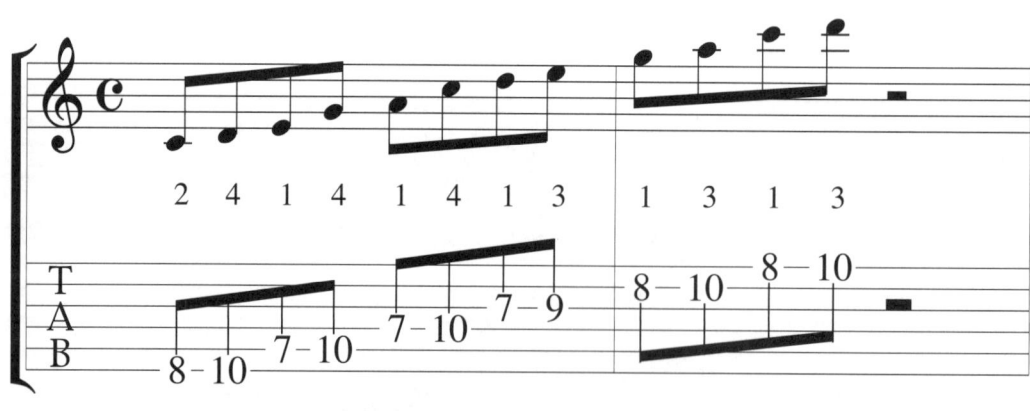

Note - The DVD markers will display on your DVD player as Title 2, Chapter 3. The title number indicates the Section and the chapter number indicates the chapter within that section. For example, all of the DVD markers in Section 2 will display as 2.14, etc. (Section 2, chapter 14). The markers in Section 3 will display as 3.12, etc. (Section 3, chapter 12).

TIP!

Practice scales slowly at first and then speed them up as you become more comfortable with them.

A BLUES SCALE - 1ST POSITION

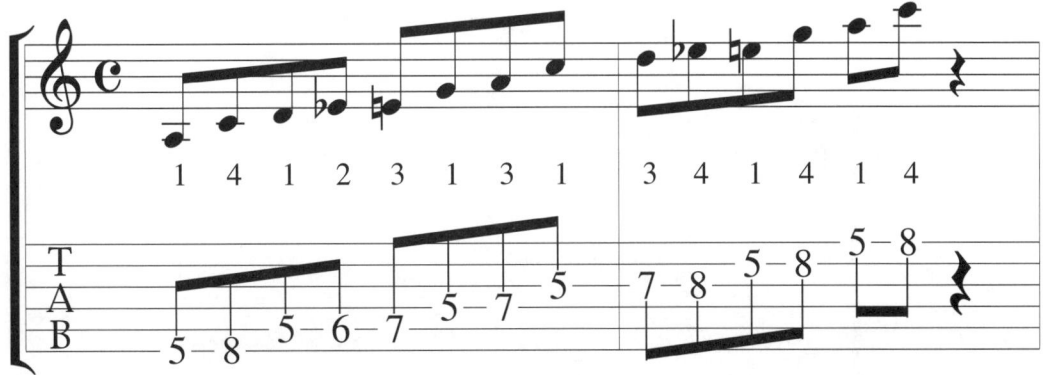

A BLUES - 2ND POSITION

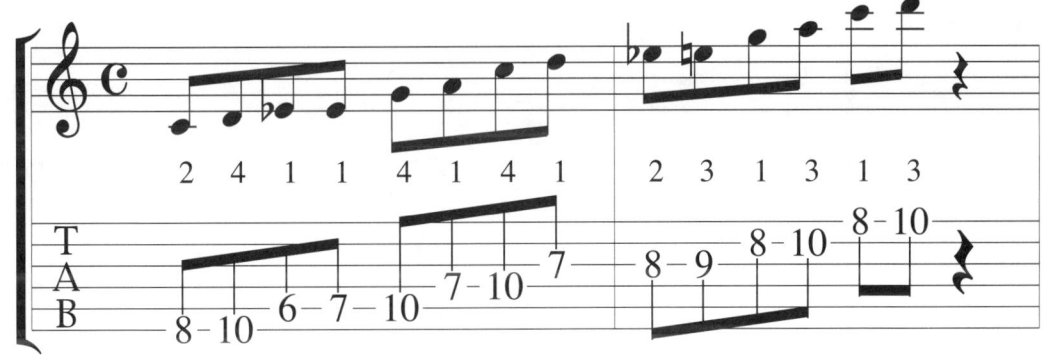

A MELODIC MINOR

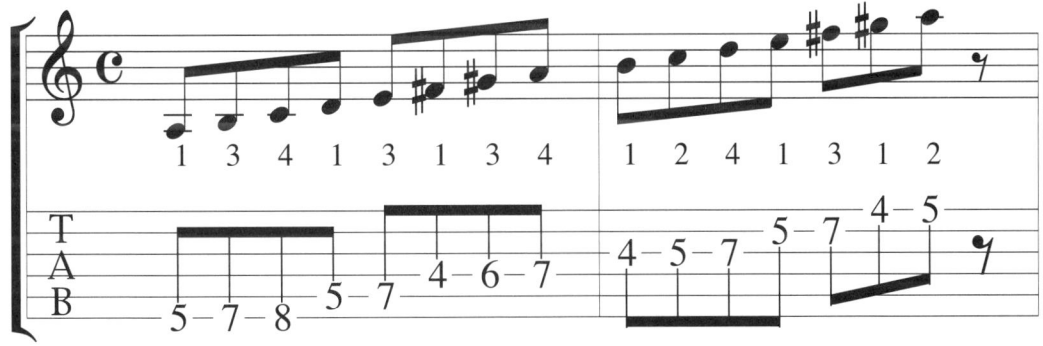

TIP!
Working with a metronome helps you practice slowly and gradually increase speed.

 LICK 1

This lick comes out of the Am pentatonic scale and starts with a simple bend, but then skips the 2nd string and plays the first. A great blues lick.

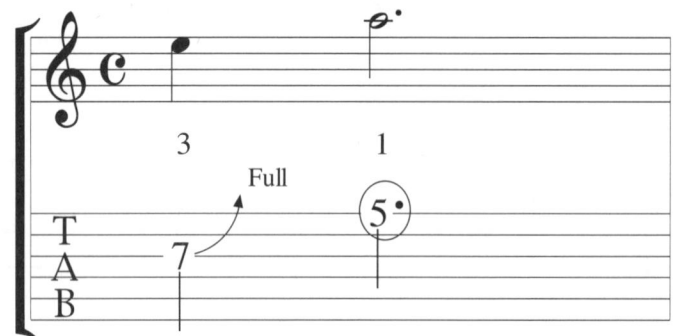

 LICK 2

This one starts the same as Lick 1, but then finishes with lower notes in the Am pentatonic scale.

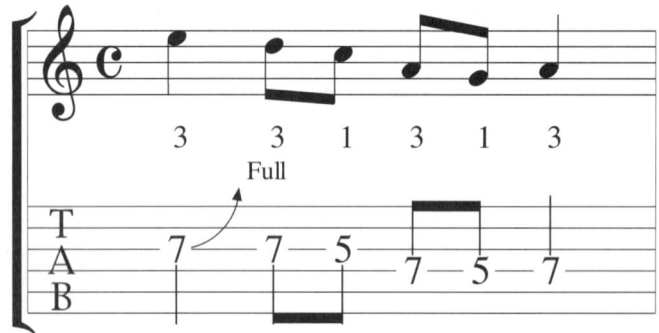

 LICK 3

This lick comes out of the Am pentatonic scale 2nd position, another cool blues lick.

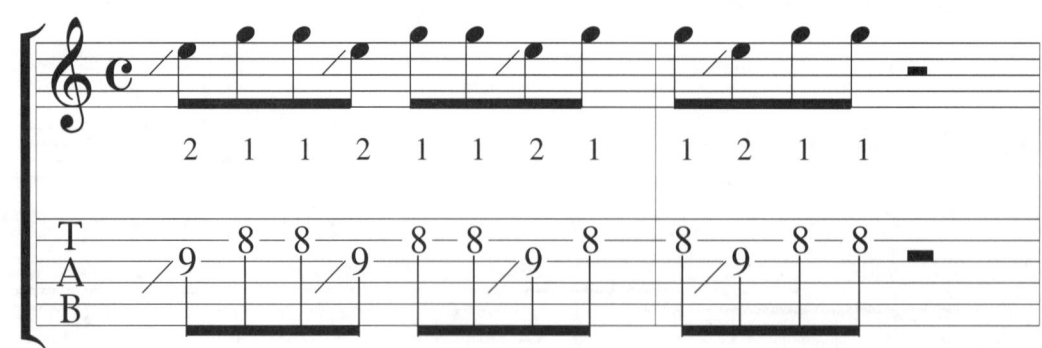

Note - There are two chapter numbers for each lick. We've put over 200 chapter markers on this DVD to make it easier to work with. The first number is the long shot intro to the lick and the second number is the split screen view of the lick being played slow and fast. You can use the Chapter Repeat button on your DVD to play just the music over & over to practice along with.

TIP!
Pay close attention to fingerings. The provided fingerings are designed to help you learn faster.

 ## LICK 4

Lick 4 comes from the A blues scale 2nd position. It phrases nicely.

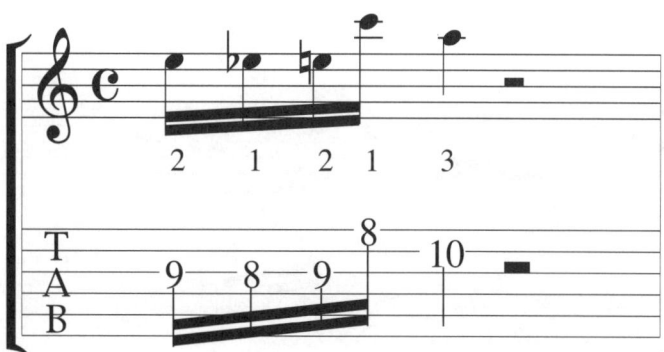

 ## LICK 5

Lick 5 is a lick out of the Am pentatonic scale 1st position. Make sure the bends get up to pitch.

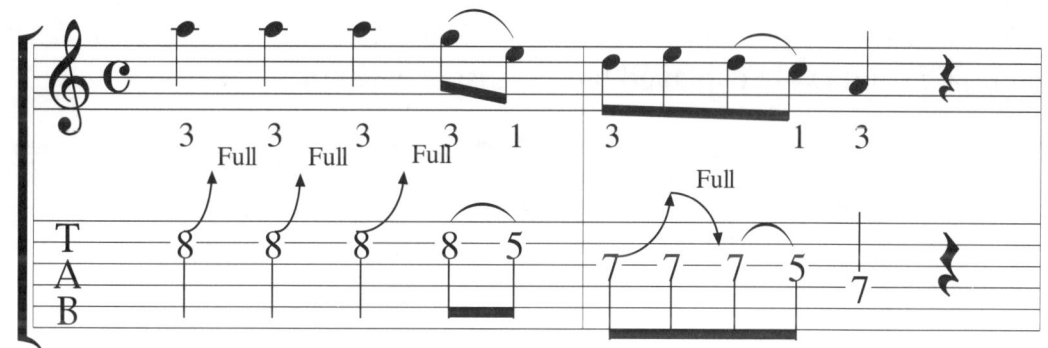

 ## LICK 6

Here's an Am pentatonic lick that starts with a bend at the 8th fret.

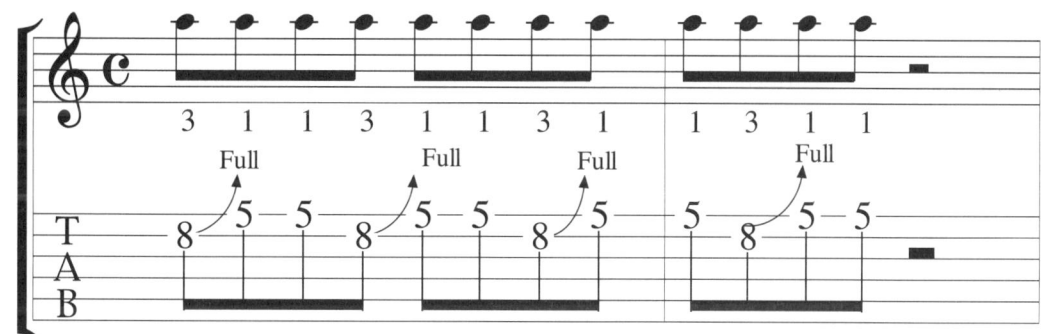

If you're having trouble with techniques in these licks such as pull offs or hammer ons, try the *Intro to Blues Guitar* or *Intro To Rock Guitar* Book & DVD. They both give clear directions on how to execute these techniques.

TIP!
Keep the strings on your guitar fresh. Change them every 2 months or sooner. The guitar will stay in tune better.

 LICK 7

This lick comes out of the A blues scale 2nd position. The slow version on the audio CD and on the DVD is played half as fast as written. Watch the hammer ons and pull offs.

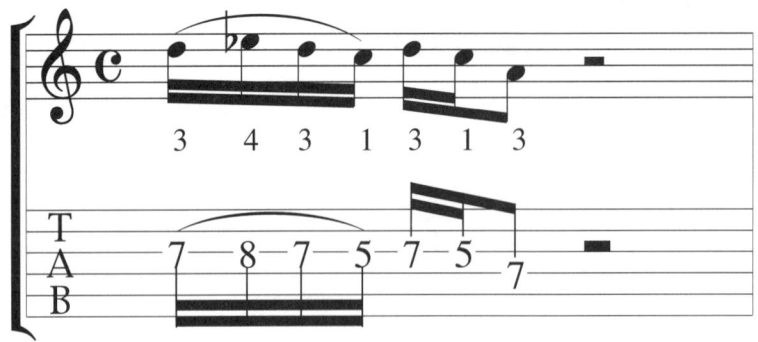

LICK 8

Here is a similar lick out of the A blues scale 2nd position. The slow version on the audio CD and DVD is played half as fast as written.

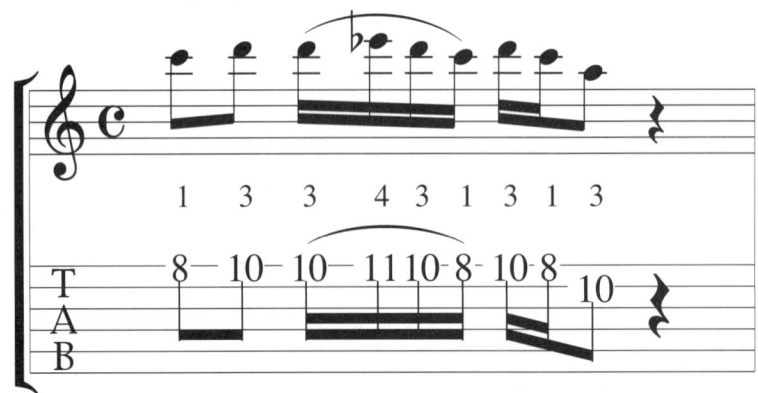

LICK 9

This lick comes out of the A blues scale 1st position. The slow version on the audio CD and DVD is played half as fast as written.

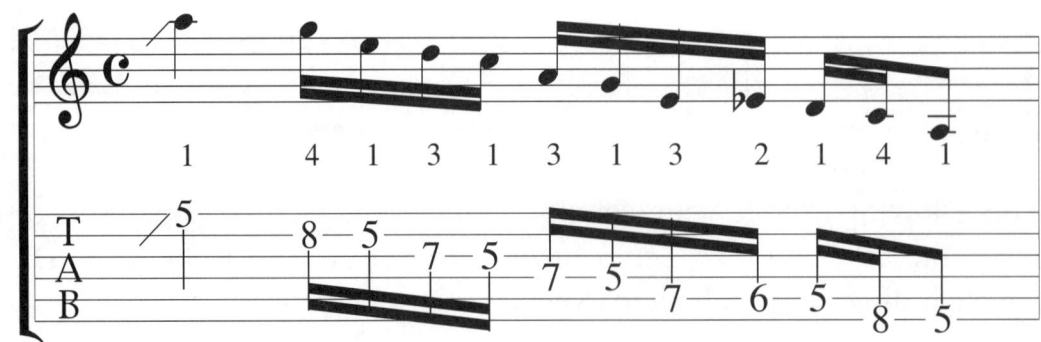

TIP!
Don't leave your guitar in extreme heat or cold. Damage may occur.

 # LICK 10

Lick 10 is a blues lick with a slightly different twist. Watch the hammer ons and pull offs and notice the blues note is on the second string. The slow version on the audio CD and DVD is played half as fast as written.

 # LICK 11

This lick comes out of the A melodic minor scale. The slow version on the audio CD and DVD is played half as fast as written. I think of it as a bebop lick.

THE EFFECTS OPTION

Try playing Lick 11 using a clean sound with some chorus added. It will give it a watery, smooth sound.

TIP! You can buy different single effects pedals or multi effects in one unit.

 LICK 12

Here is a lick using octaves and the Am pentatonic scale. With the right hand, you can use either a pick or thumb to play both strings with a strumming motion. You must mute the string in between with your left hand index finger.

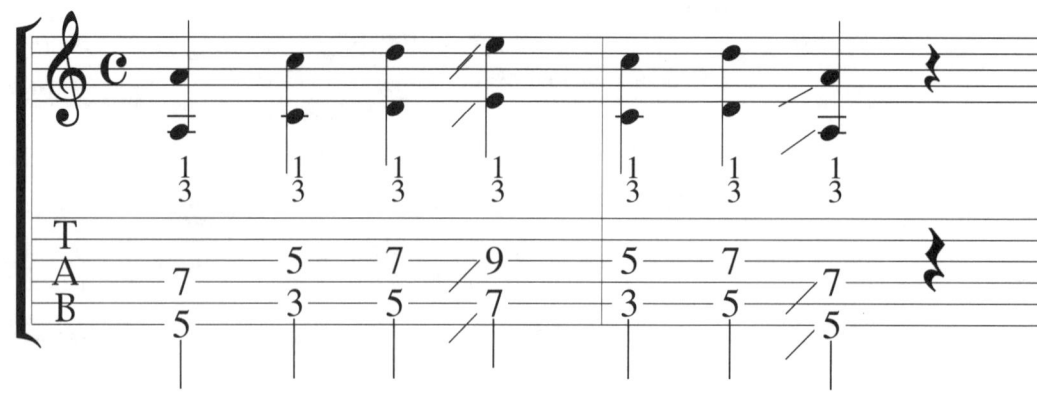

 LICK 13

This lick starts with a Em arpeggio and uses the A minor scale. An arpeggio is playing one note of a chord at a time. For more on arpeggios, go to the Appendix.

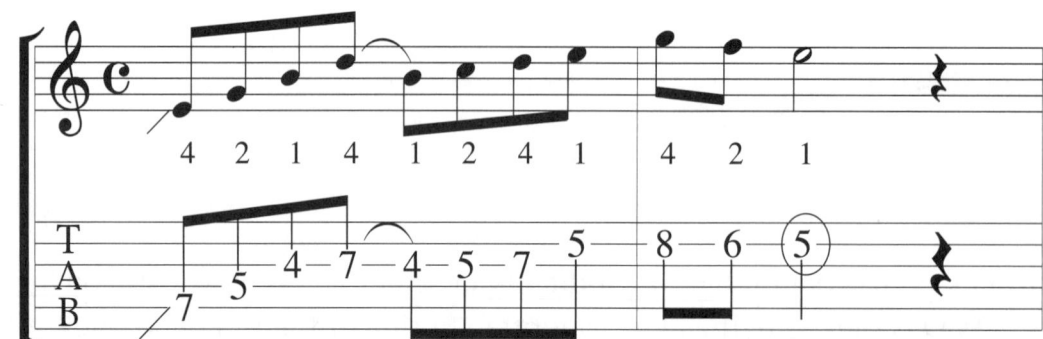

 LICK 14

Here's a lick out of the A minor scale 1st position. It starts with an Am7 arpeggio. The slow version on the audio CD and on the DVD is played half as fast as written.

TIP!
A good guitar teacher can speed up your improvement by 200 to 300 percent.

 LICK 15

This lick is out of the A minor scale 2nd position. It starts with an Am9 arpeggio. The slow version on the audio CD and on the DVD is played half as fast as written.

PRACTICING WITH THE LET'S JAM TRACK

Included on the CD and DVD is a track with the licks played over Track 4 of the *Let's Jam! CD Blues & Rock*. This is meant to give you an example of how these licks should sound. Listen to this track, but don't necessarily try to play along with it. Once you are comfortable with several licks, try playing with the Let's Jam track provided with the CD (Track 93) or DVD (Special Features Section). This will give you a track to practice the same lick over and over. Try different phrasing and timings of the lick. Make it your own lick.

On the next two pages is a listing of the 15 licks we have learned in this section. These are placed here to make it easy to work with the licks when playing along with the Let's Jam track. The licks are played in one group of 15 on the CD and 3 groups of 5 on the DVD.

PLAYING WITH TRACK 4 - LET'S JAM! CD BLUES & ROCK

Lick 1

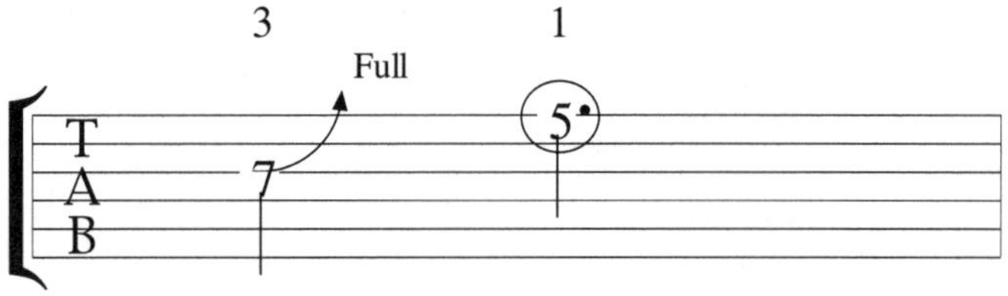

Lick 2

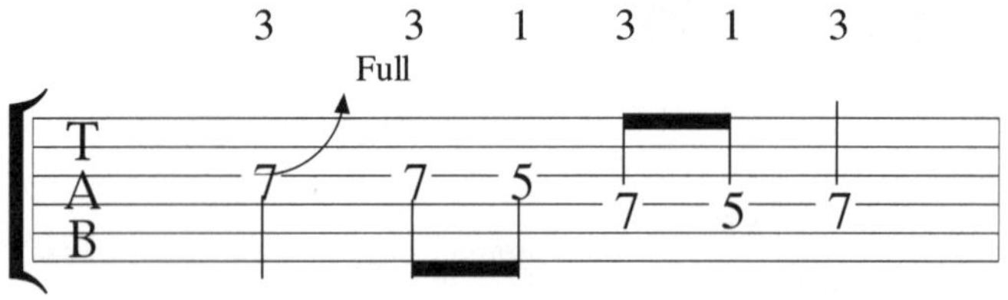

Lick 3

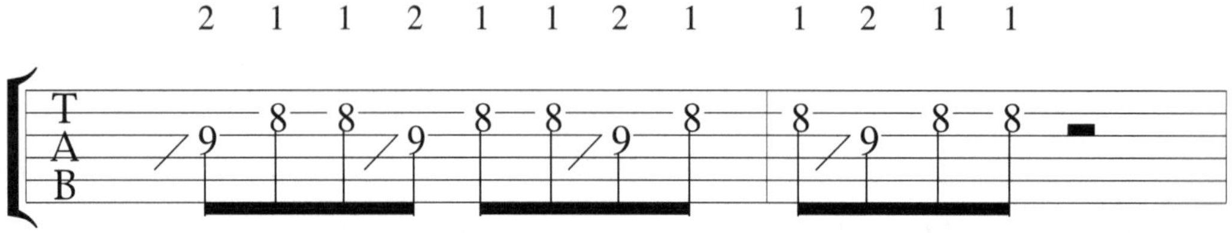

Lick 4

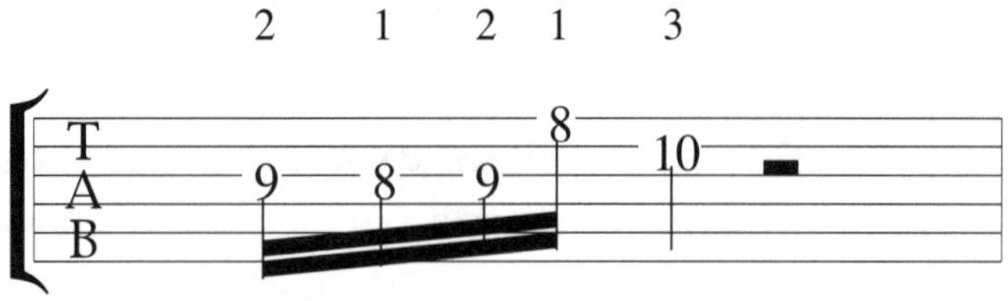

Lick 5

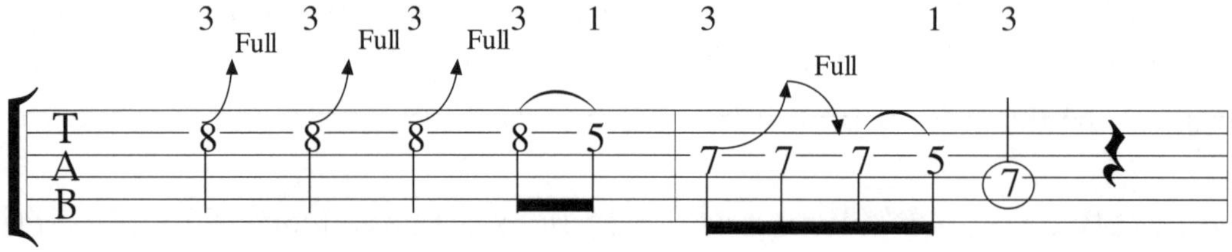

Lick 6

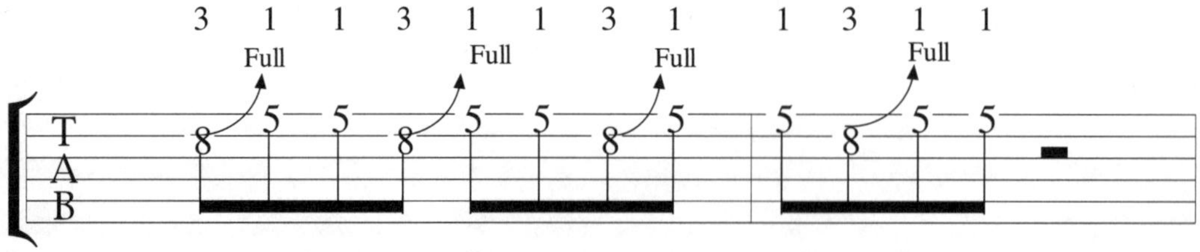

Lick 7

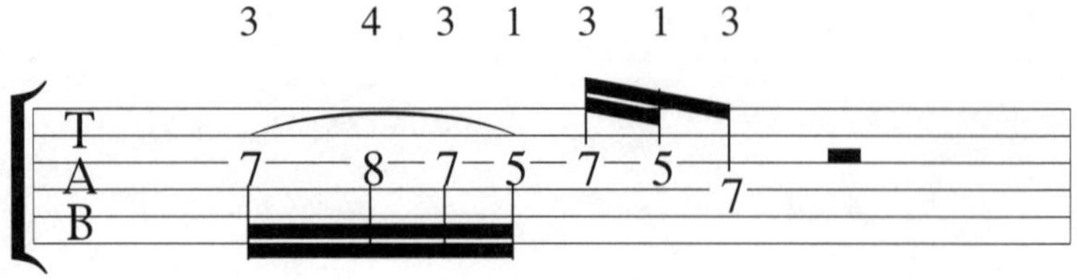

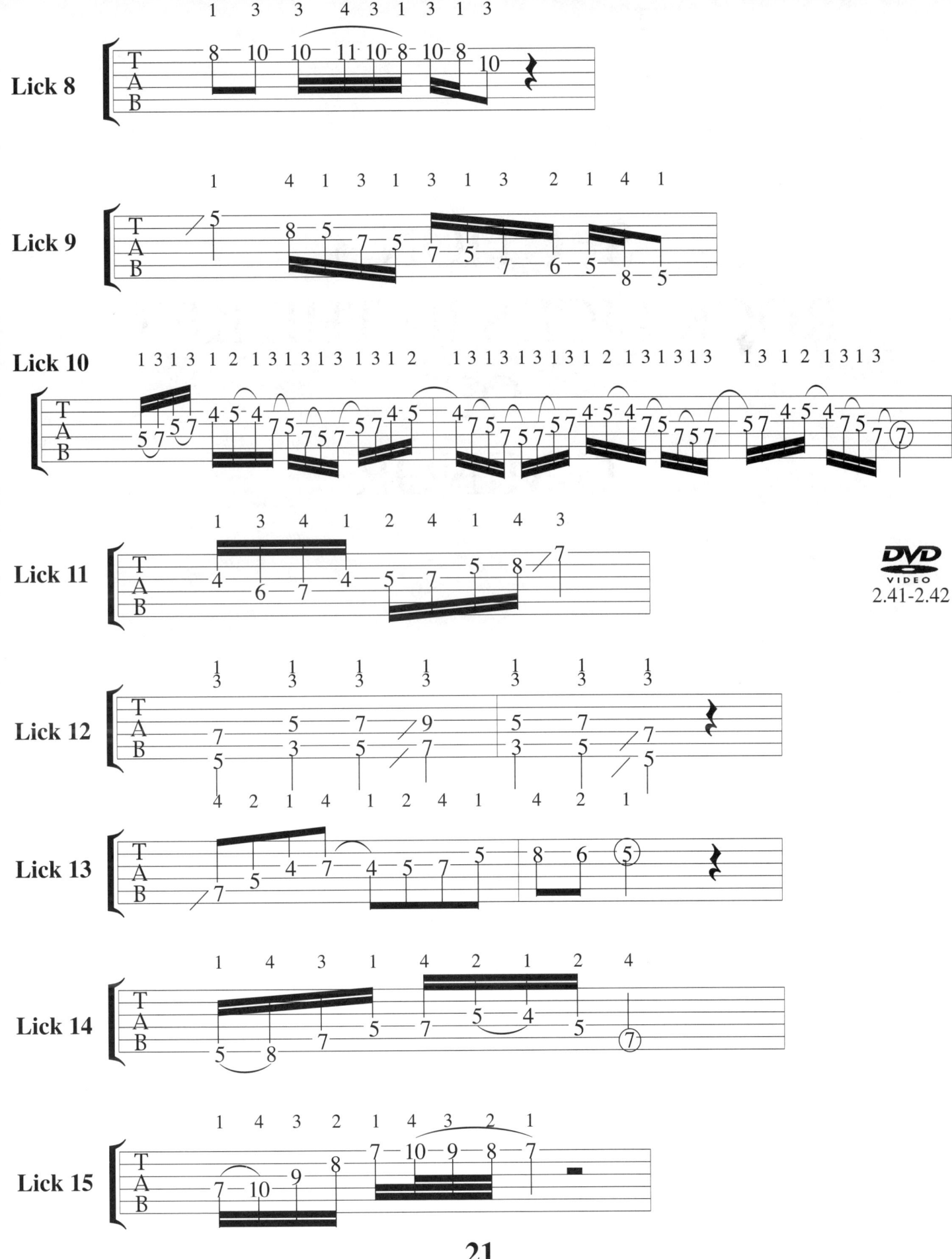

SECTION 3
ROCK LICKS IN THE KEY OF
G MINOR

The licks in this section will all be in the key of G minor. To hear what these licks sound like, we will be using Track 15 of the *Let's Jam! CD Hard Rock*, which is Track 94 on the companion CD. It is not necessary to have the *Let's Jam* CD to learn these licks, but it will prove useful as you try to use them in different keys and chord progressions. There are several scales that will be used in this section. Below are the scales and positions you will need. Become comfortable with these before going on to the licks. We are using scales from *The Guitarist's Scale Book*.

G MINOR PENTATONIC - 1ST POSITION

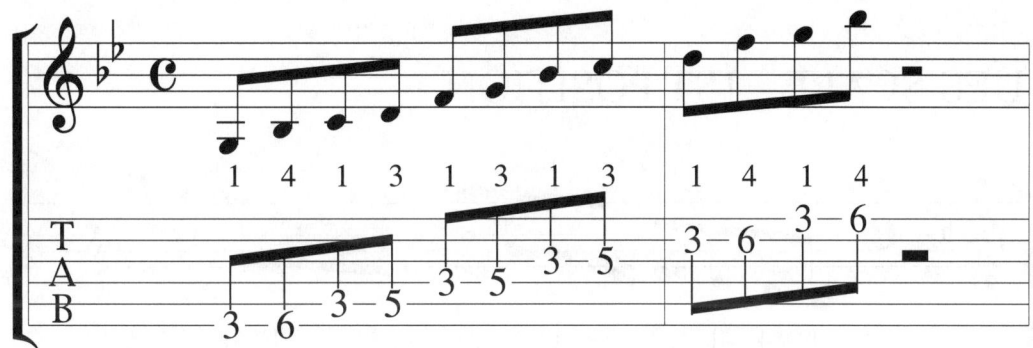

G MINOR PENTATONIC - 2ND POSITION

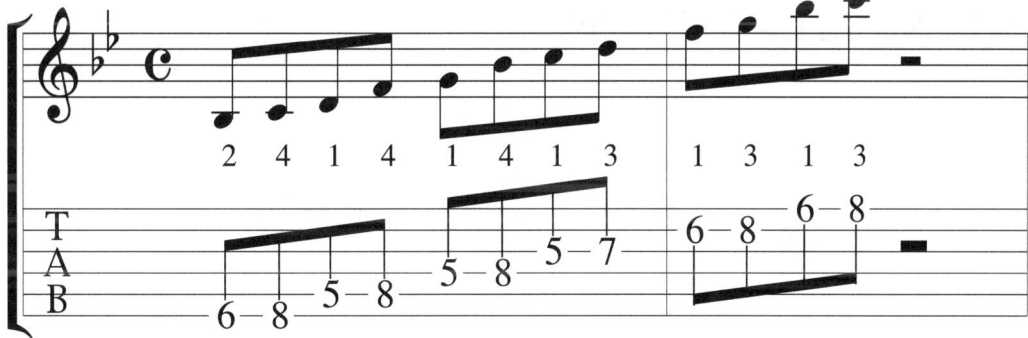

TIP!
If you're having trouble with rhythm, try a drum machine instead of a metronome. It gives you more subdivisions of the beat.

G MINOR PENTATONIC - 4TH POSITION

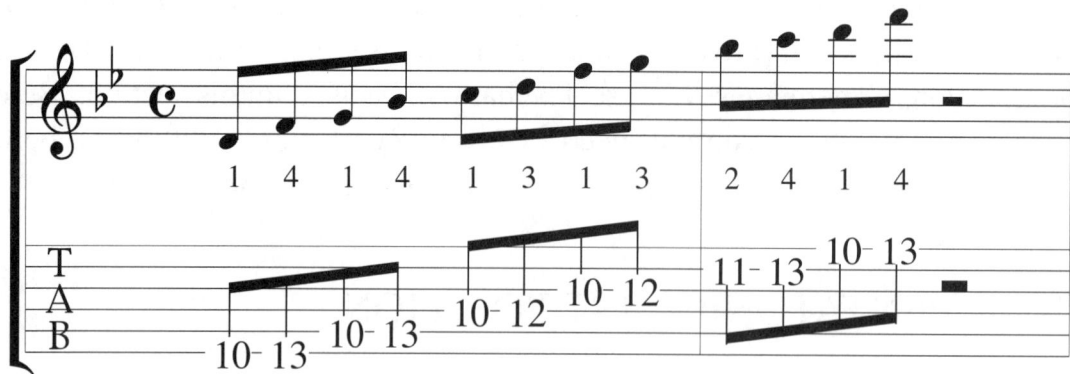

G BLUES SCALE - 1ST POSITION

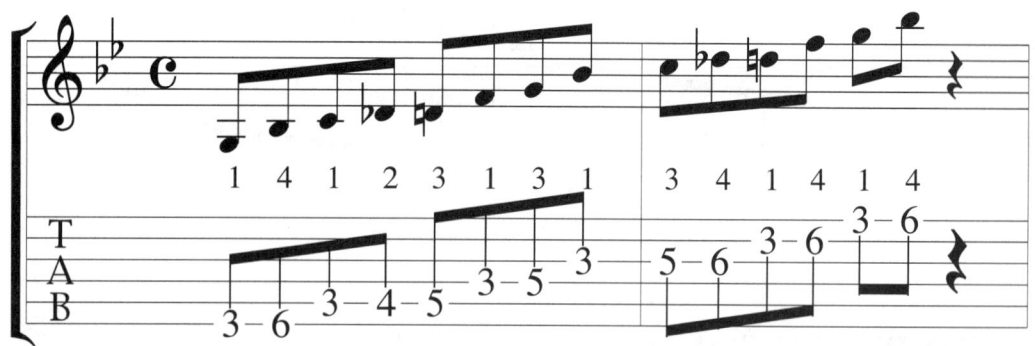

G DORIAN - 1ST POSITION

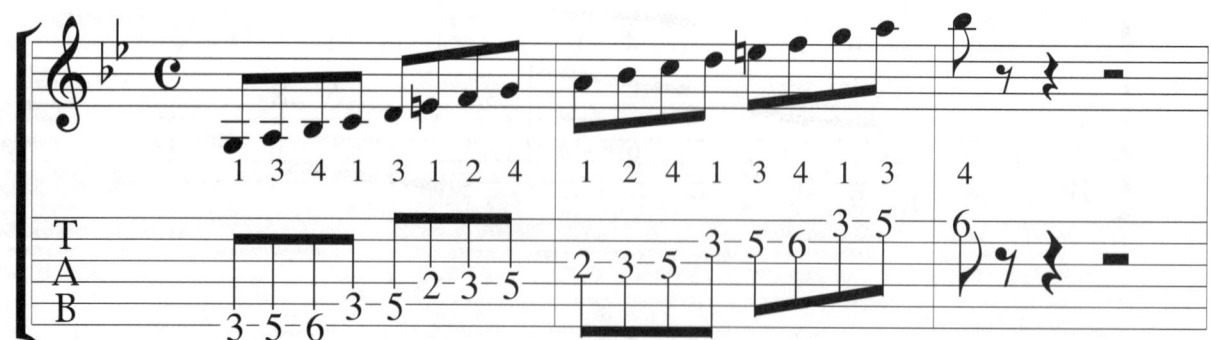

TIP!
Put lemon oil on your fretboard every couple of months when you're changing strings.

 ## LICK 1

3.7-3.8

This lick comes out of Gm pentatonic 1st position. Make sure the bend gets up to pitch.

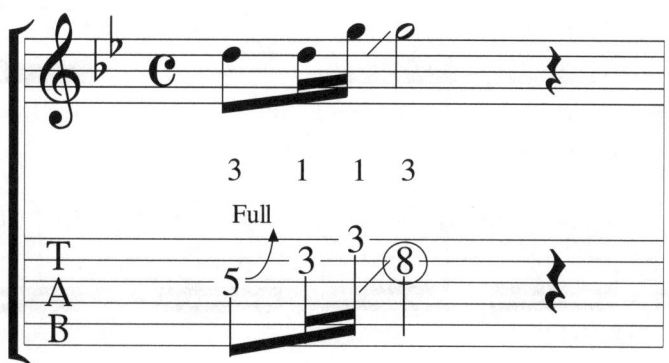

LICK 2

3.9-3.10

Similar to Lick 1, but this time with double stops. The slow version on the audio CD and the DVD is played half as fast as written. Play this entire lick with down-strokes with your pick.

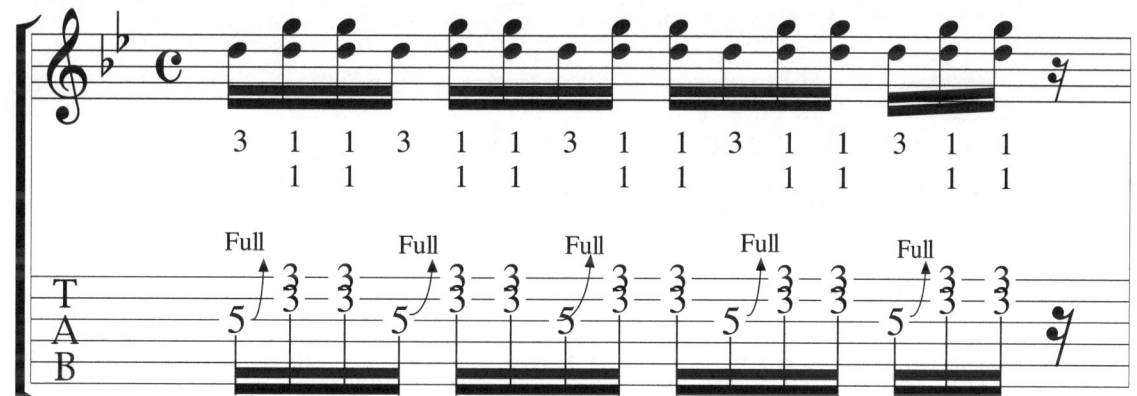

 ## LICK 3

3.11-3.12

Again out of Gm pentatonic 1st position. Make sure the bend is accurate.

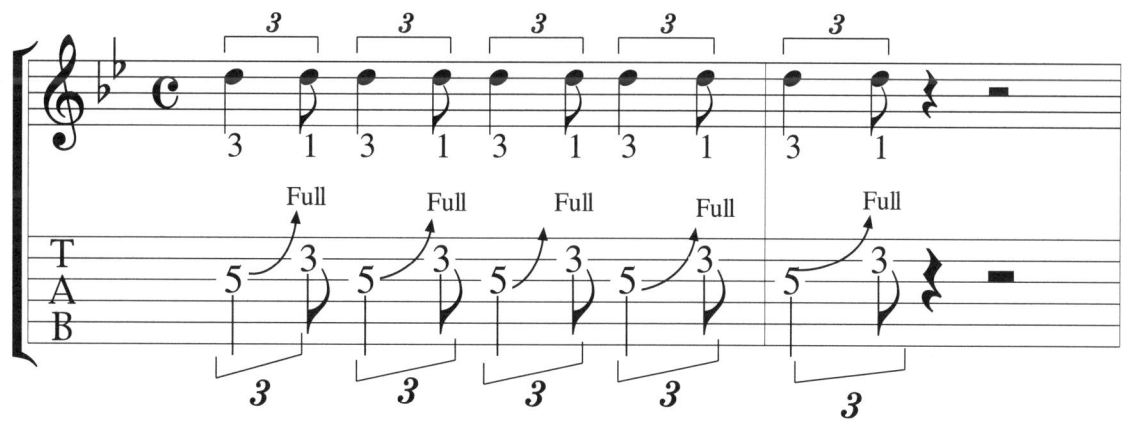

TIP!
Have your guitar set up twice a year and it will play easier and more in tune.

 ## LICK 4

A classic rock and roll lick. Watch the pull offs.

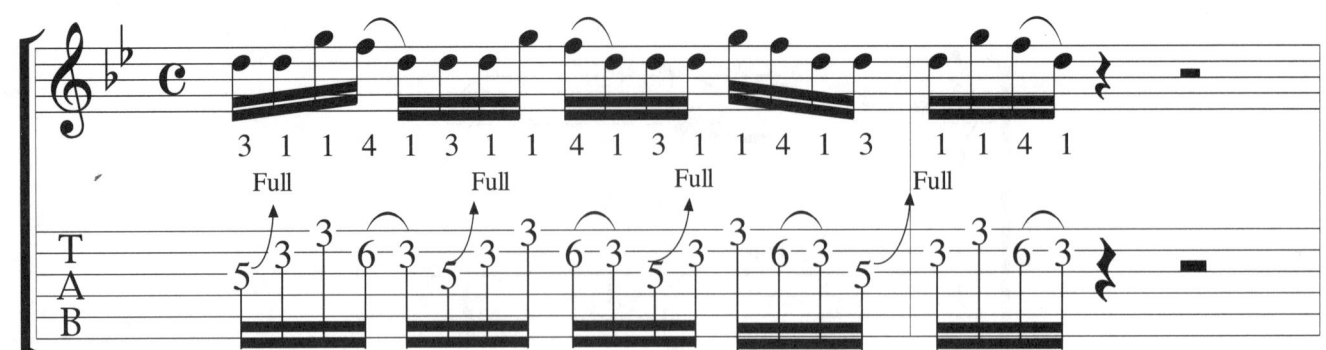

 ## LICK 5

This lick is basically a trill in Gm.

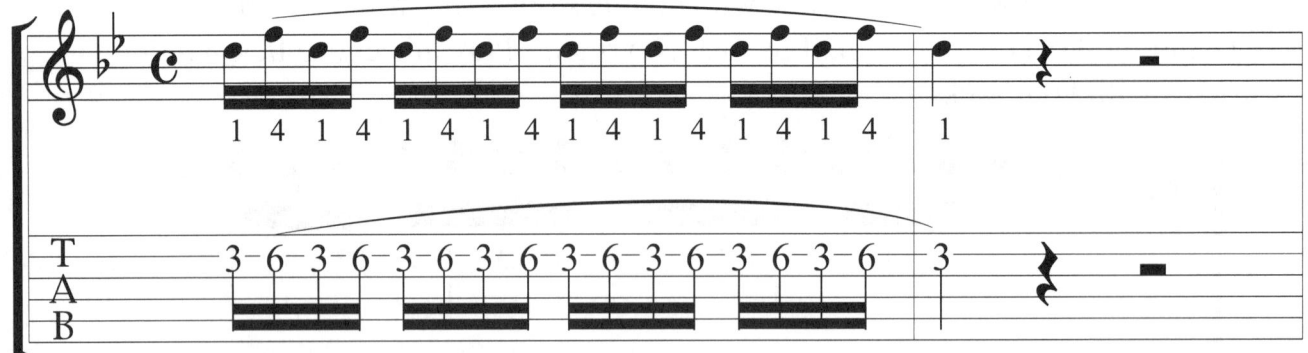

THE EFFECTS OPTION

Try playing Lick 5 using a phaser or flanger effect. Listen to the CD or DVD to hear what this sounds like. Check with your local music store to see what effects pedals are available.

 ## LICK 6

1st position Gm pentatonic starting with hammer ons.

TIP!
If you're going to stand when performing, you should occasionally practice while standing.

LICK 7

Here's a lick alternating bends using artificial harmonics. Artificial harmonics are made by touching the string with a finger of your right hand at the same time you're picking that string. This creates a higher note. Listen to the audio example on the CD or DVD to get a better idea of what an artificial harmonic should sound like.

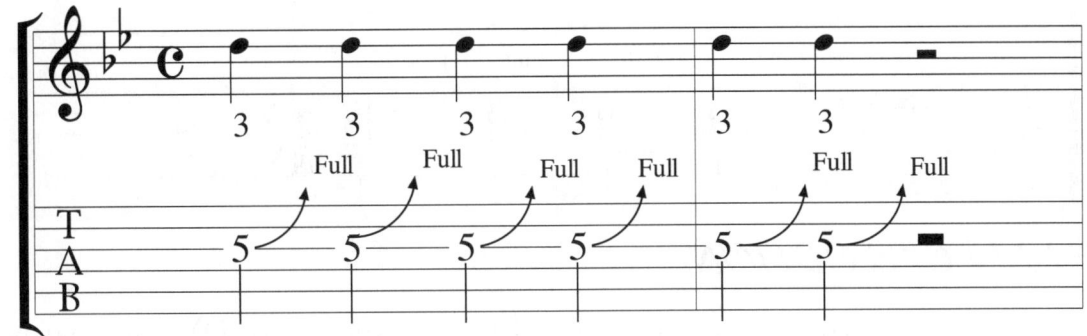

LICK 8

A lick using pull offs to open strings. Big fun.

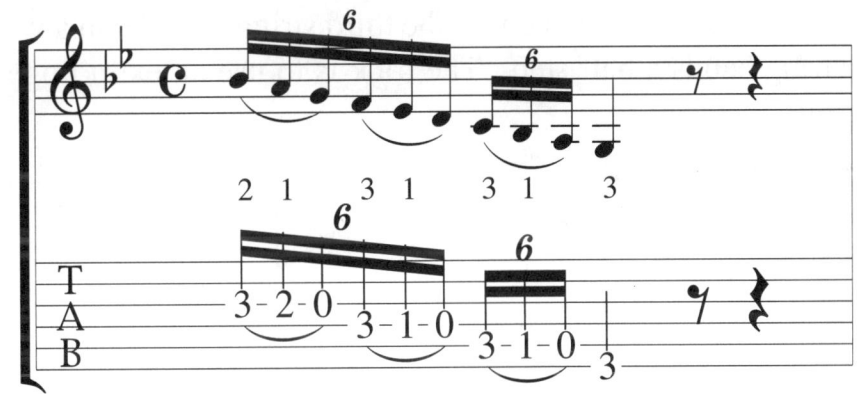

LICK 9

Here's another lick using pull offs and open strings. This lick uses the Gm scale.

TIP!
Practice your licks and techniques with a clean sound more often than with distortion. It will help you be more precise.

27

 ## LICK 10

This is a lick moving up the Gm scale. Unisons are created by bending the third string.

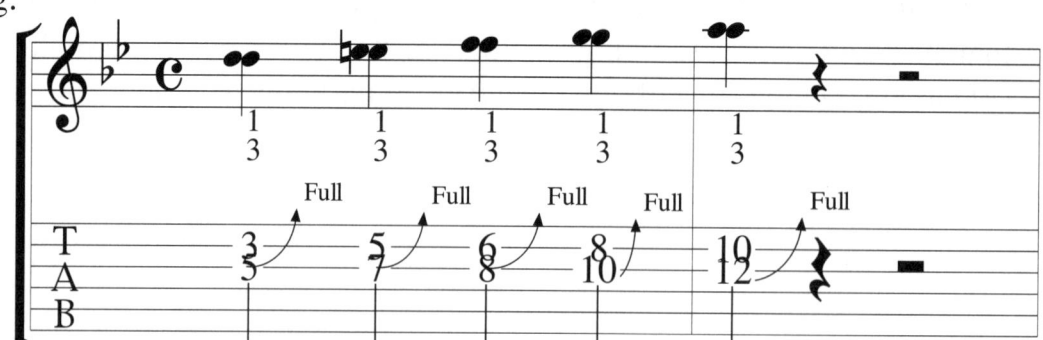

 ## THE EFFECTS OPTION

Try playing Lick 10 using a wah pedal. Listen to the CD or DVD to hear what this sounds like.

 ## LICK 11

Here is a tricky double stop bend. The third string must bend a whole step while the second string bends a half step. The trick is to use an extra finger to help bend the third string.

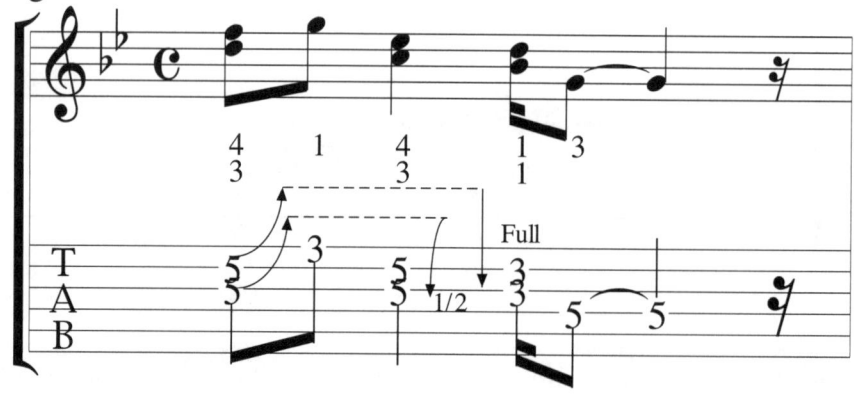

 ## LICK 12

A lick using the 4th position Gm pentatonic scale. Watch the pull off and slide.

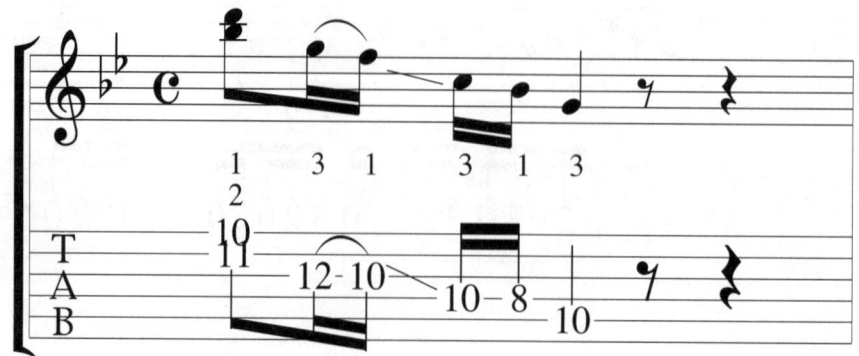

TIP!
Standard effects used by guitar players include chorus, distortion, digital delay, and wah pedals.

 ## LICK 13

A lick using the G blues scale 1st position. Watch the combination hammer on pull off.

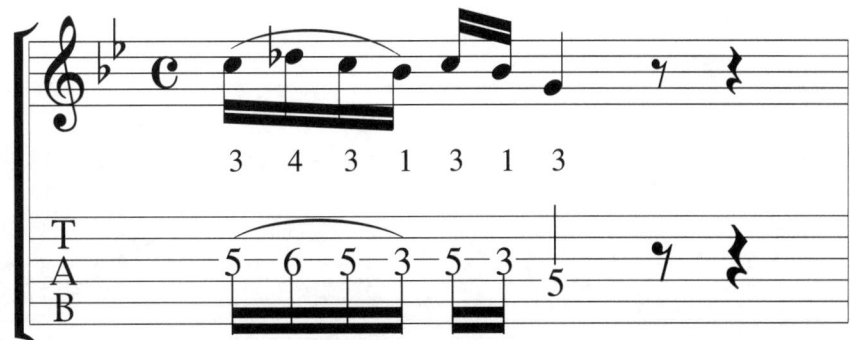

 ## LICK 14

A combination G Dorian and G blues lick. A hand friendly lick.

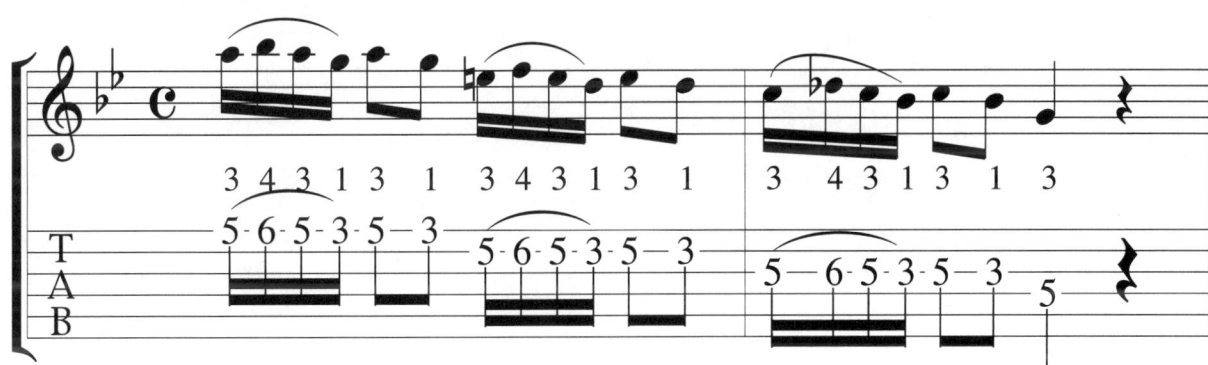

 ## LICK 15

This lick is a G blues lick coming out of 3rd position of the G blues scale.

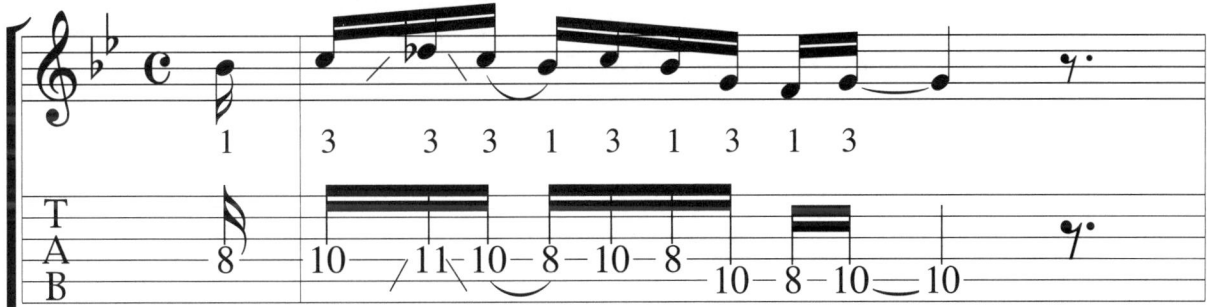

 ### THE EFFECTS OPTION

Try playing Lick 15 using an octaver pedal. Listen to the CD or DVD to hear what this sounds like.

TIP!
If you don't understand terms like Dorian or Mixolydian, get a teacher that knows theory or buy the Guitarist's Scale Book, which has a great explanation of the modes.

CD 40

PLAYING WITH TRACK 15 - LET'S JAM! CD HARD ROCK

DVD VIDEO 3.40-3.41

Lick 1

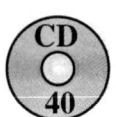

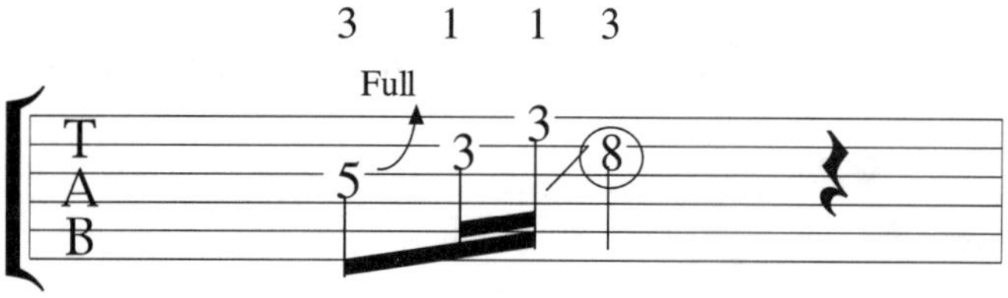

Lick 2

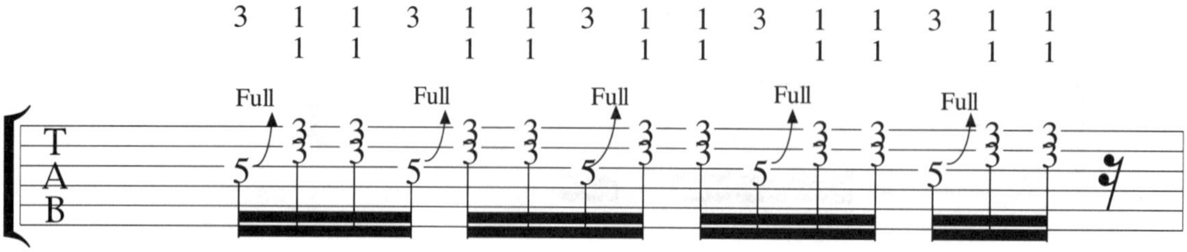

Lick 3

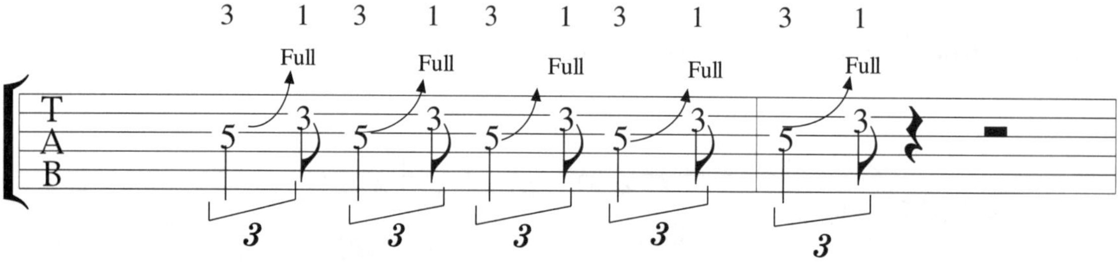

Lick 4

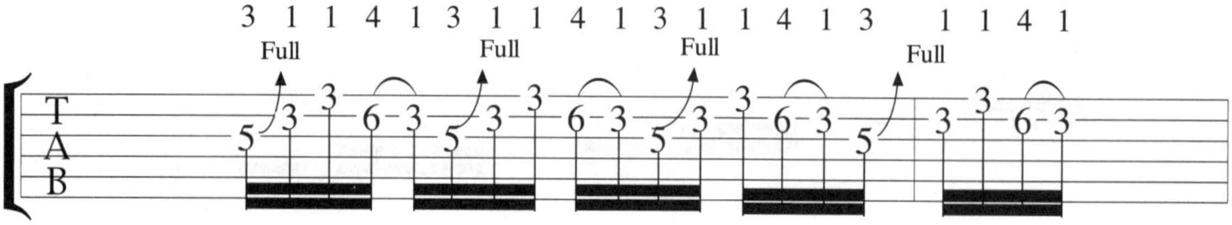

Lick 5

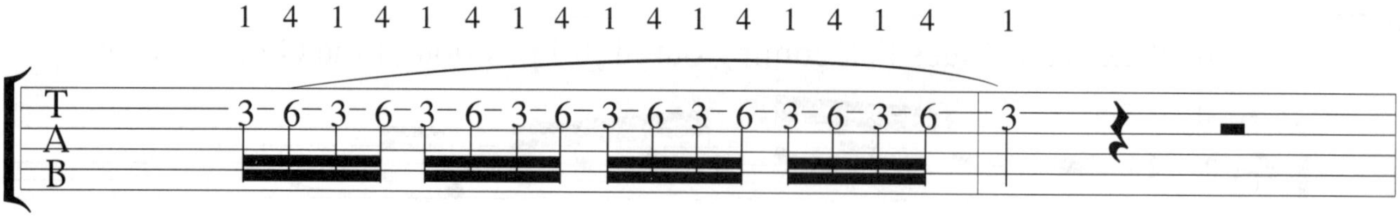

Lick 6

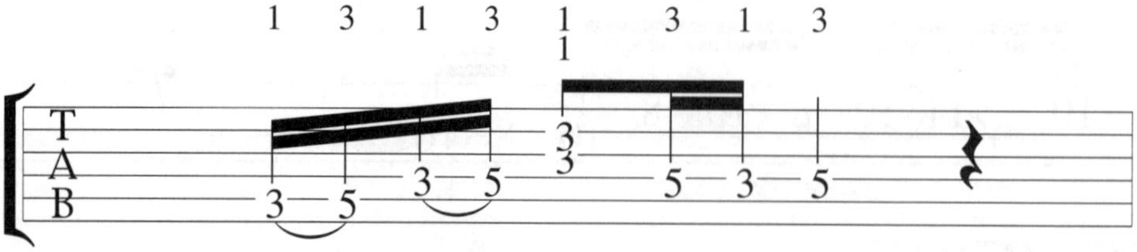

DVD VIDEO 3.42-3.43

Lick 7

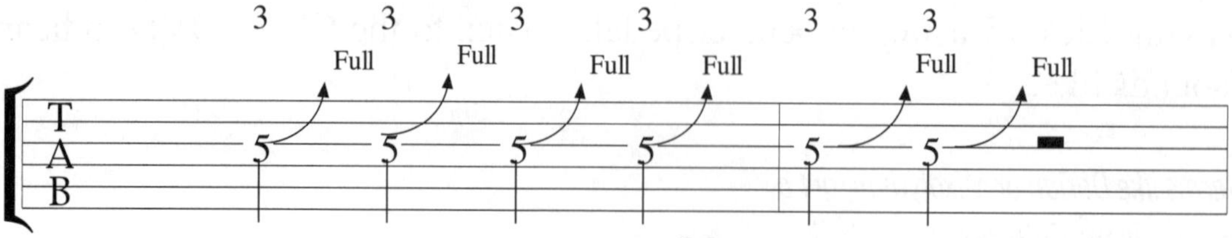

SECTION 4
BLUES LICKS IN THE KEY OF A

The licks in this section will all be in the key of A major. To hear what these licks sound like, we will be using Track 4 of the *Let's Jam! CD Blues & Jazz*, which is Track 95 on the companion CD. It is not necessary to have the *Let's Jam* CD to learn these licks, but it will prove useful as you try to use them in different keys and chord progressions. There are several scales that will be used in this section. Below are the scales and positions you will need. Become comfortable with these before going on to the licks. These scale positions are taken from *The Guitarist's Scale Book*.

A BLUES WITH A MAJOR THIRD

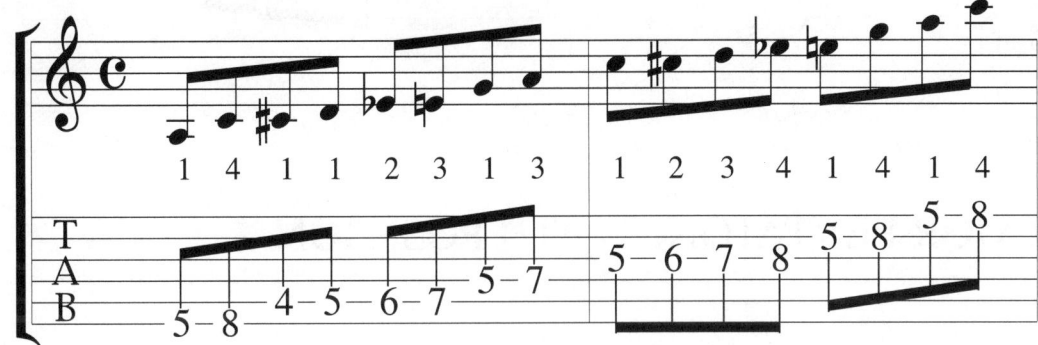

A MINOR PENTATONIC - 2ND POSITION WITH MAJ 3RD

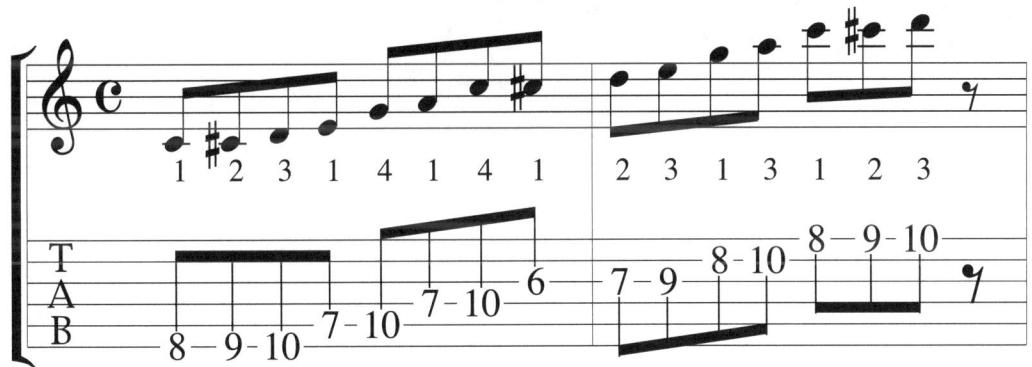

A MINOR PENTATONIC - 4TH POSITION

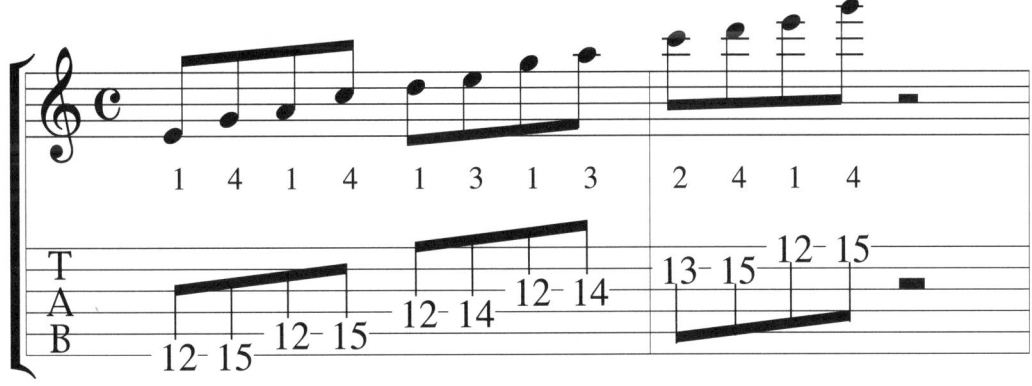

TIP!
If your tube amplifier is making noises, it may need new tubes. Have it checked out.

A MAJOR PENTATONIC

A MAJOR PENTATONIC - 4TH POSITION

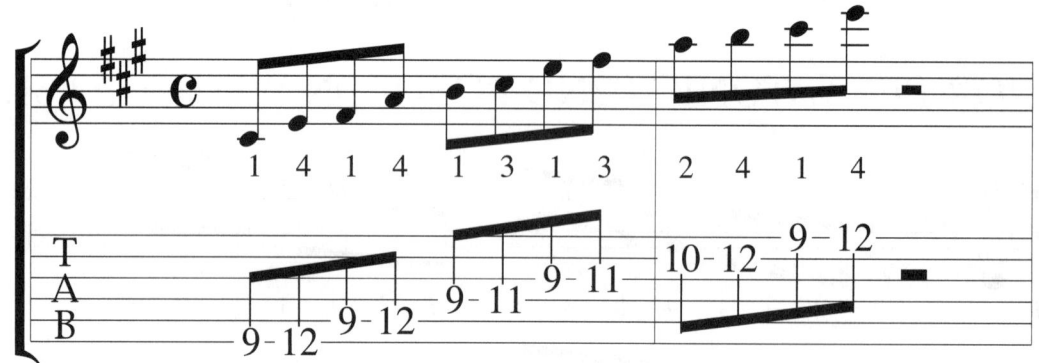

A MIXOLYDIAN

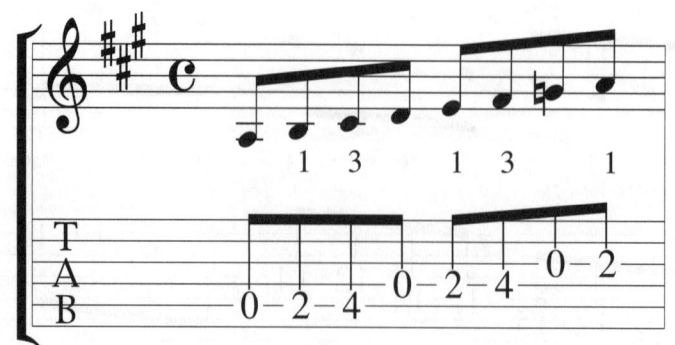

TIP!
When first starting to play, warm up slowly so you won't injure yourself.

 ## LICK 1

This lick comes out of the Am pentatonic scale, but includes the major 3rd. It's a standard blues lick that can be used in a major key. It's also played with a swing feel. This means the 8th notes aren't even. Listen to the audio CD to get a better idea of how this should sound.

 ## LICK 2

Here's a lick that comes out of a combination of A blues and Am pentatonic, again with the major 3rd.

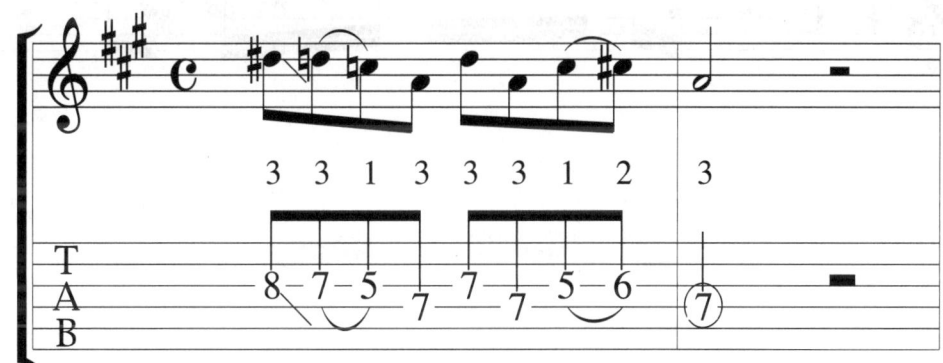

 ## LICK 3

Here's a great example of a blues lick with both the minor and major third.

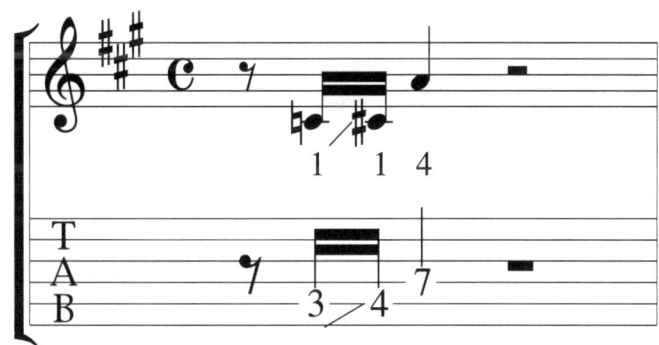

TIP!

Keep your wrists, forearms, and elbows in good shape. Try a weight lifting regimen. Use light weights at first and talk to your doctor to avoid injuries.

 ## LICK 4

This is a lick using the A blues scale and the major third.

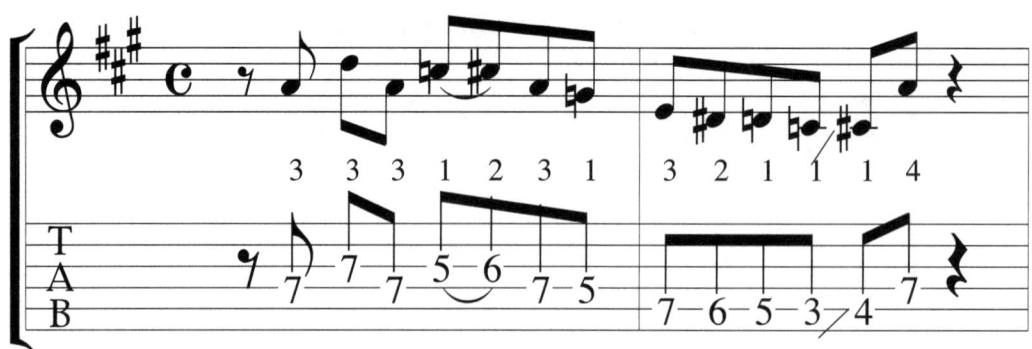

 ## LICK 5

Again a combination of major and minor pentatonic. Watch the slides.

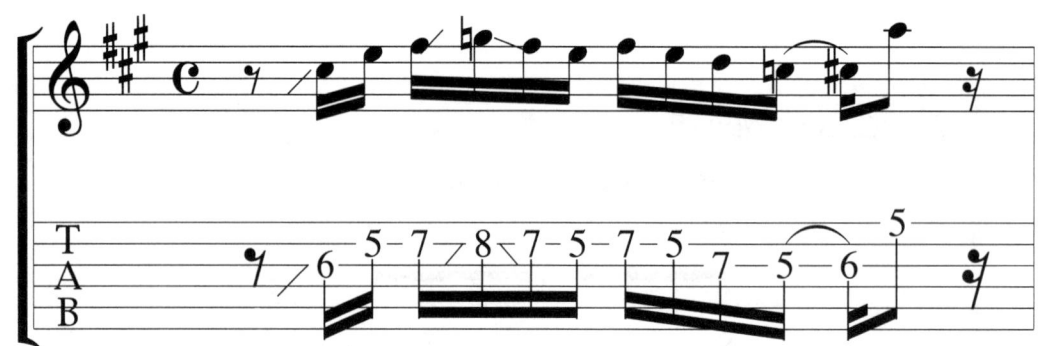

 ## LICK 6

Lick 6 uses the A blues scale.

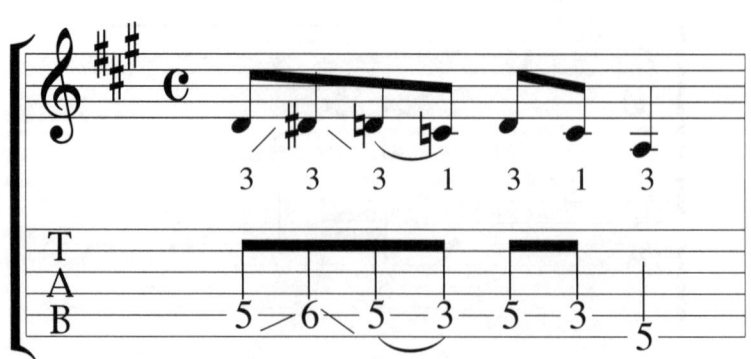

TIP!
Take short breaks when practicing to allow your hands and arms to relax.

 ## LICK 7

This lick comes out of the 2nd position A minor pentatonic scale and uses the major 3rd.

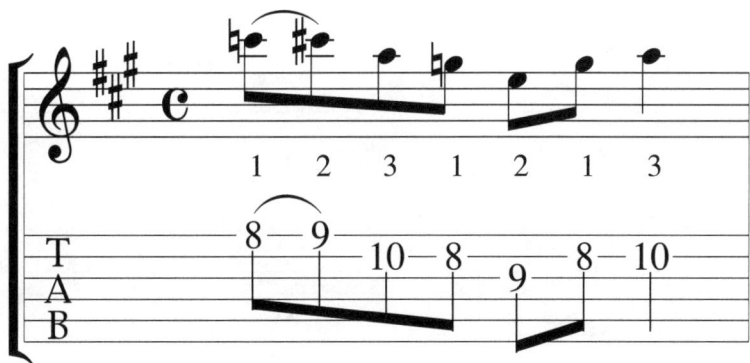

 ## LICK 8

Here is a combination A major and A minor pentatonic. Mostly it is centered around the 4th position A major pentatonic.

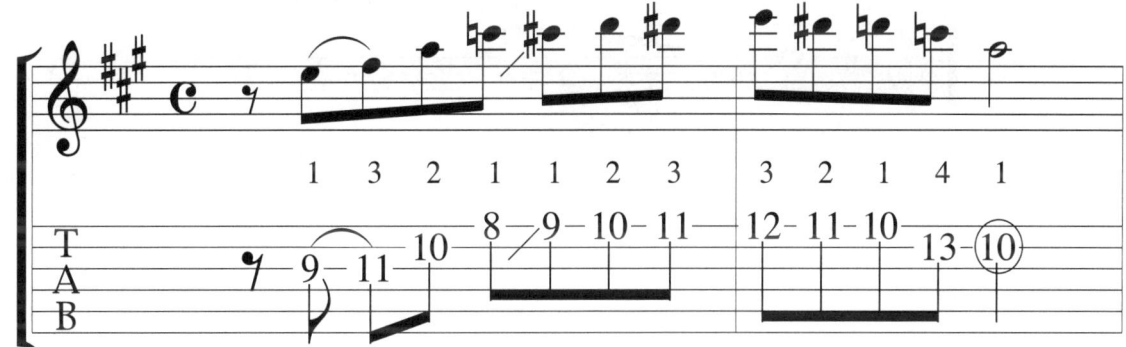

 ## LICK 9

Again a combination of major and minor pentatonic. It starts in the 4th position A minor pentatonic.

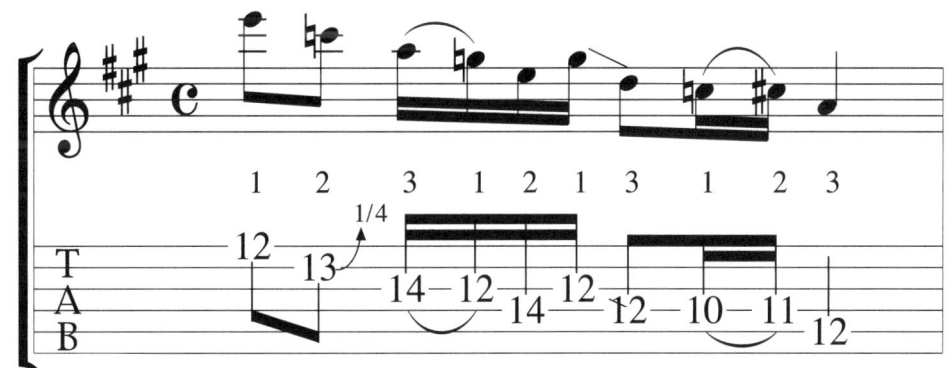

TIP!
Keep an emergency strap and cable in your car in case you need one unexpectedly.

 ## LICK 10

This lick comes out of A major pentatonic. Watch the bends.

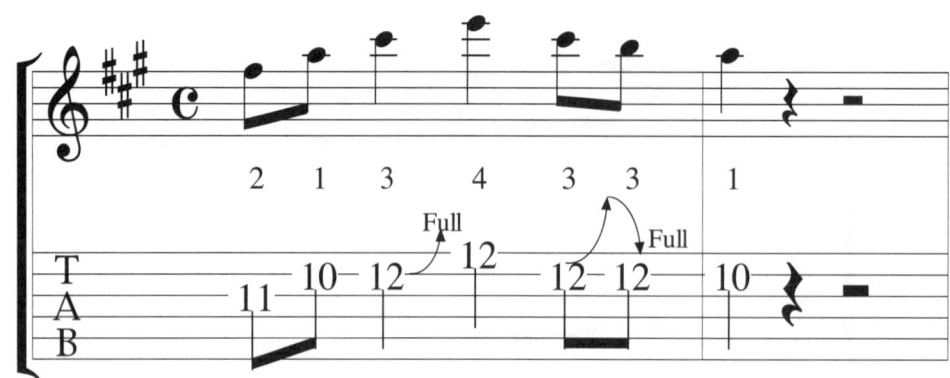

 ## LICK 11

Again a combination of major and minor pentatonic. Make sure the bend is accurate.

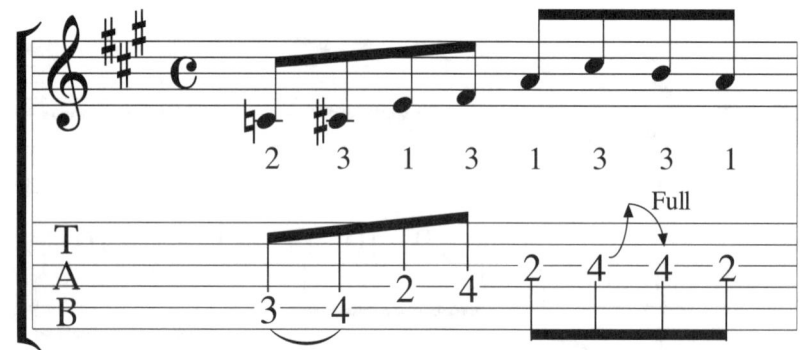

 ## LICK 12

Here's a lick that is chromatic, meaning it moves by half step, and uses an F# minor arpeggio. For more on arpeggios, go to the Appendix.

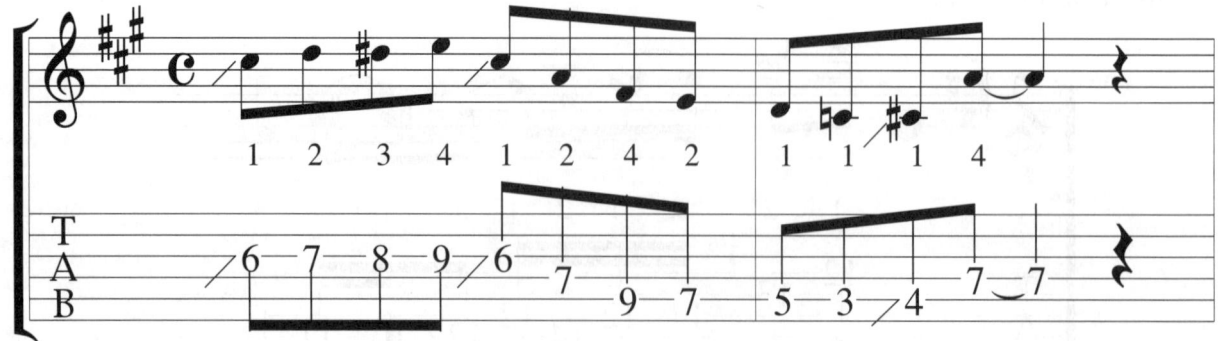

TIP!
Jam along CDs such as the Let's Jam series are great ways to try out new licks and scales.

 ## LICK 13

This lick can be thought of a couple ways. It is an A Mixolydian lick or can be thought of as using A major pentatonic and the open strings.

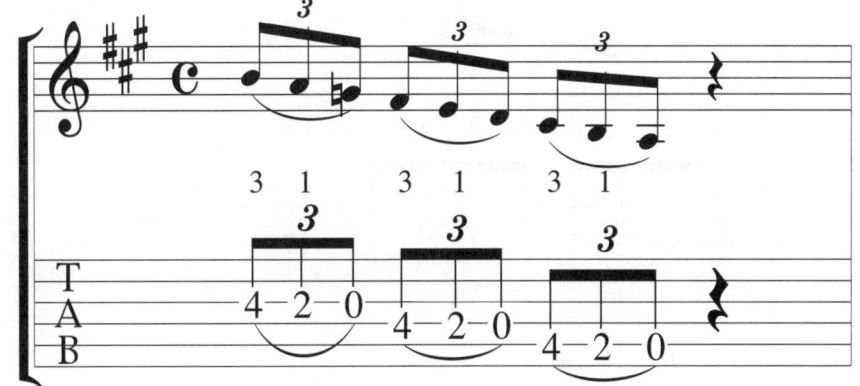

 ### THE EFFECTS OPTION

Try playing Lick 13 using a harmonist pedal. Listen to the CD or DVD to hear what this sounds like.

LICK 14

Here are some double stops. The lick uses the A major pentatonic scale and chromatic notes.

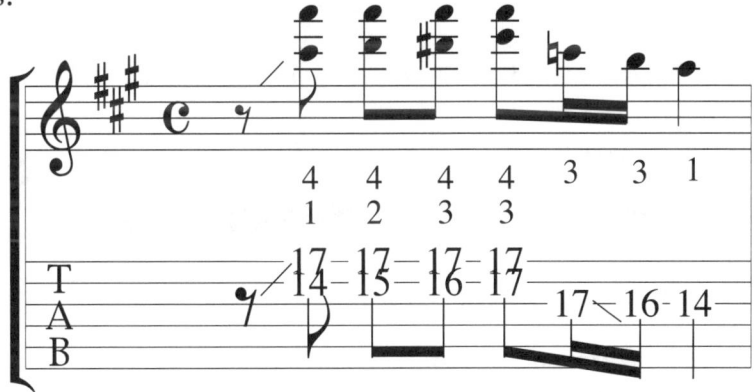

LICK 15

This is a double stop lick using a combination of Am and A major pentatonic.

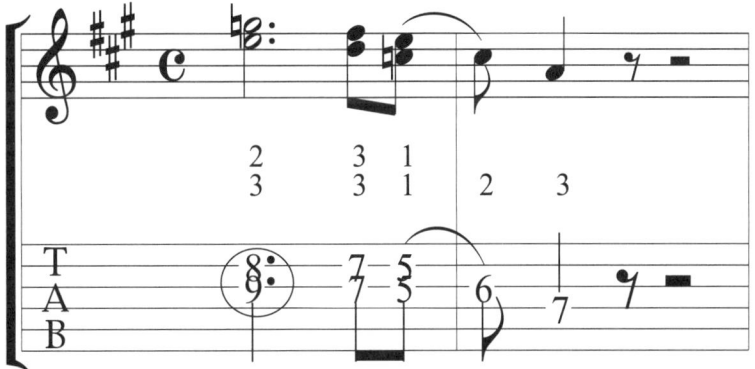

TIP!
Use an electronic tuner to stay in good tune. They are inexpensive and user friendly.

PLAYING WITH TRACK 4 LET'S JAM! CD JAZZ & BLUES

Lick 1

Lick 2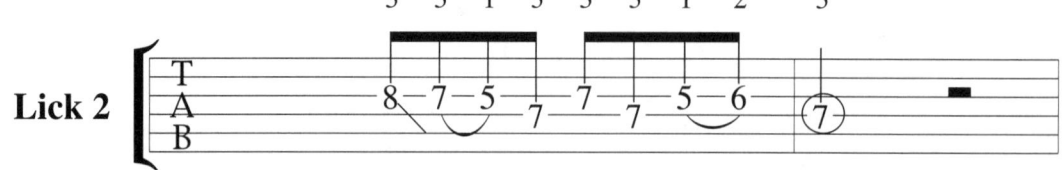

Lick 3

Lick 4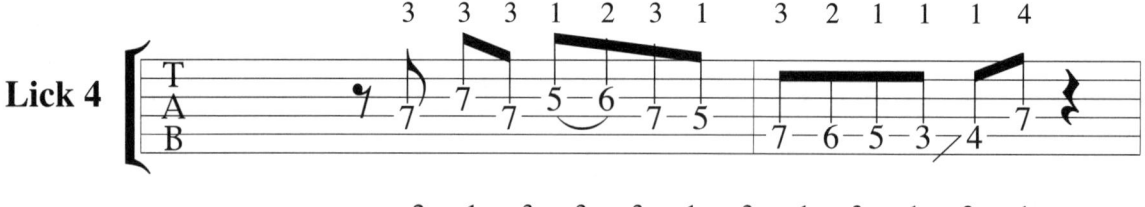

Lick 5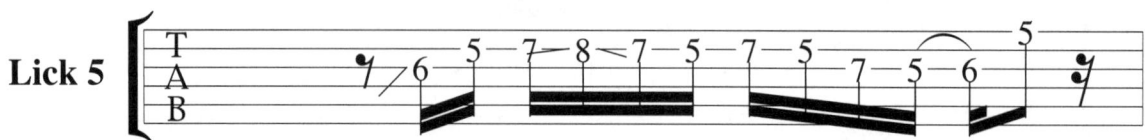

Lick 6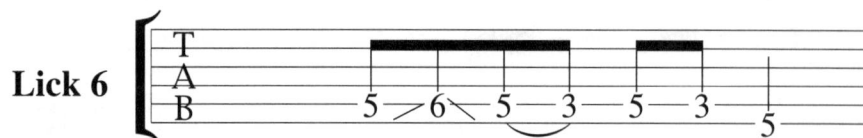

Lick 7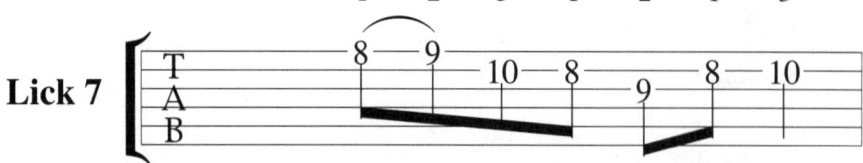

Lick 8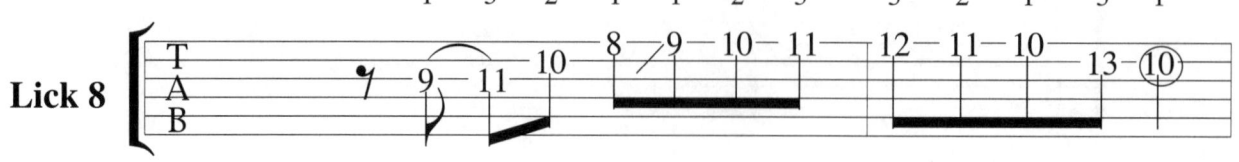

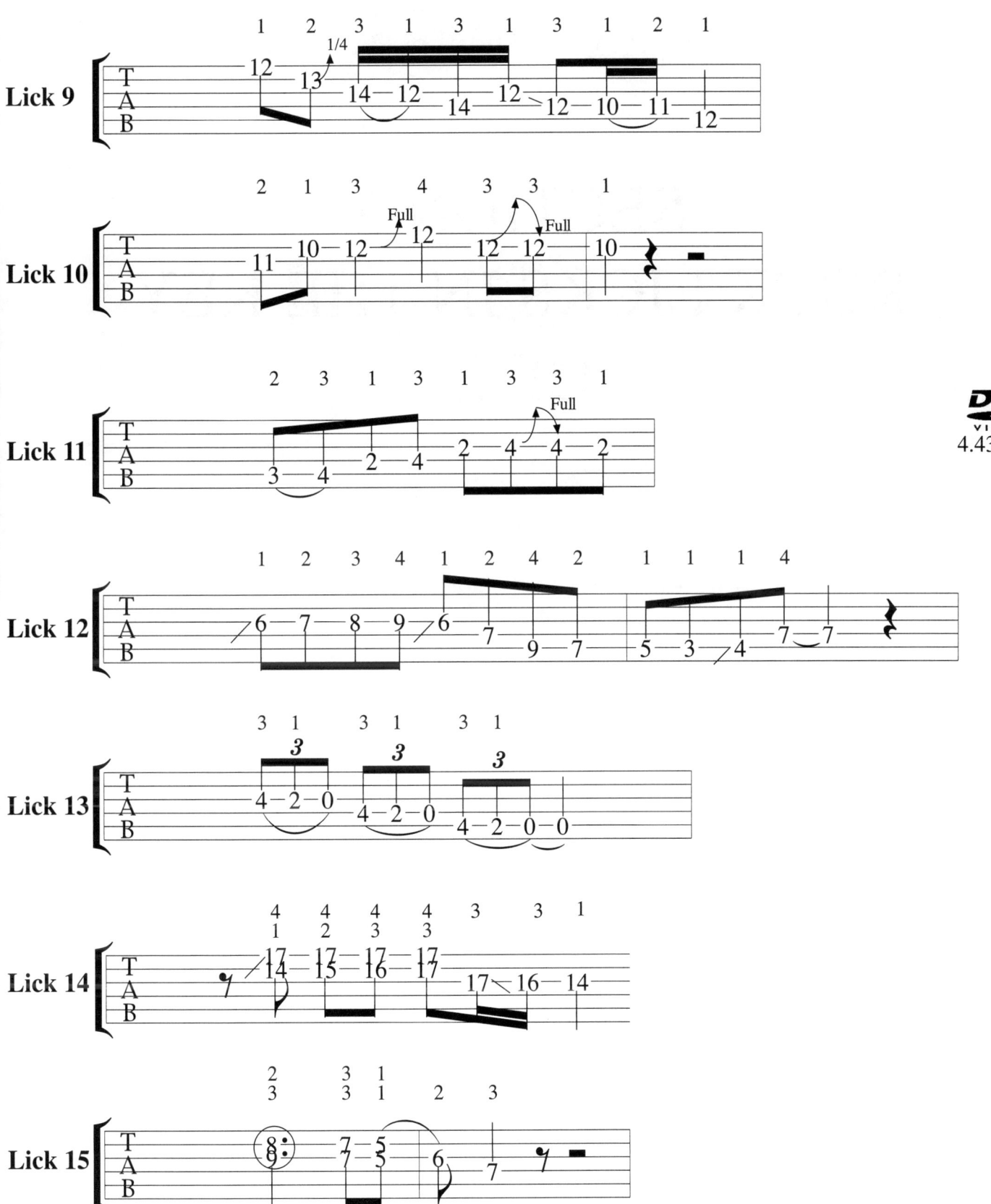

SECTION 5
ROCK LICKS IN THE KEY OF E

The licks in this section will all be in the key of E major. To hear what these licks sound like, we will be using Track 5 of the *Let's Jam! CD Hard Rock*, which is Track 96 on the companion CD. It is not necessary to have the *Let's Jam* CD to learn these licks, but it will prove useful as you try to use them in different keys and chord progressions. There are several scales that will be used in this section. Below are the scales and positions you will need. Become comfortable with these before going on to the licks. We are using scale positions from *The Guitarist's Scale Book*.

E BLUES

E MINOR PENTATONIC - 12TH FRET

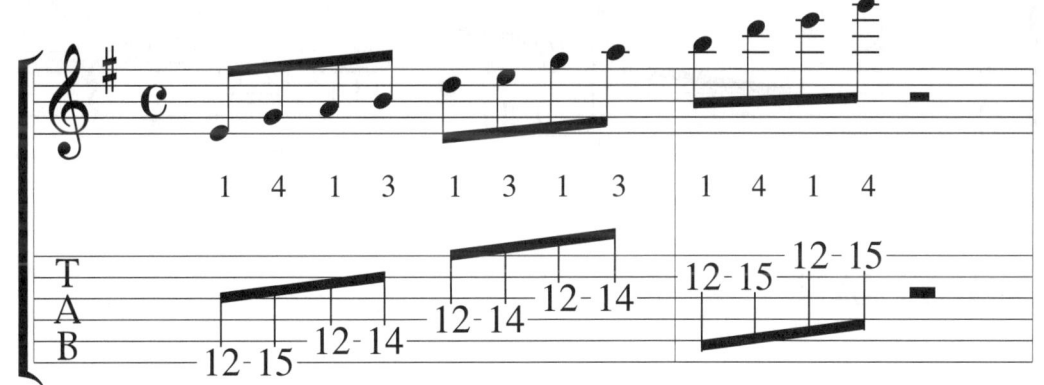

E MAJOR PENTATONIC - 1ST POSITION

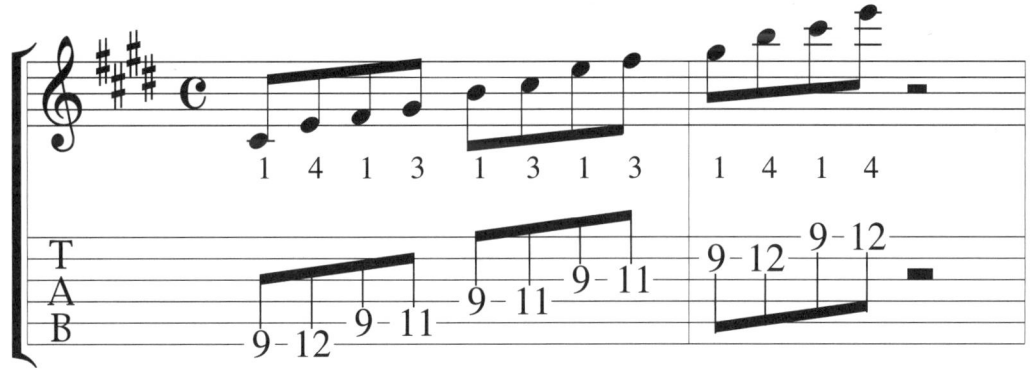

TIP!
Keep many extra picks around. They like to disappear, much like socks.

43

E MAJOR PENTATONIC - 4TH POSITION

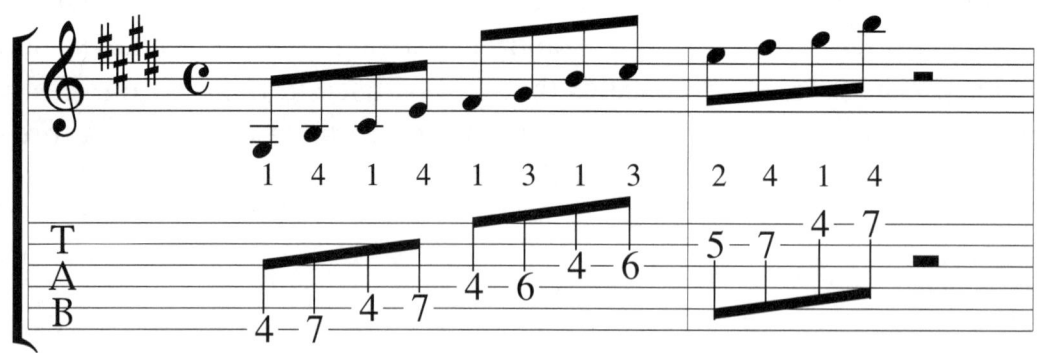

E MAJOR PENTATONIC - EXTENDED

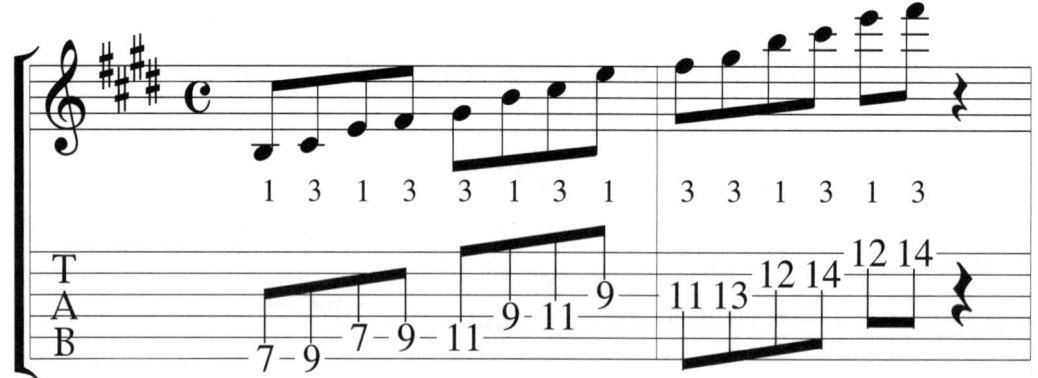

E MIXOLYDIAN

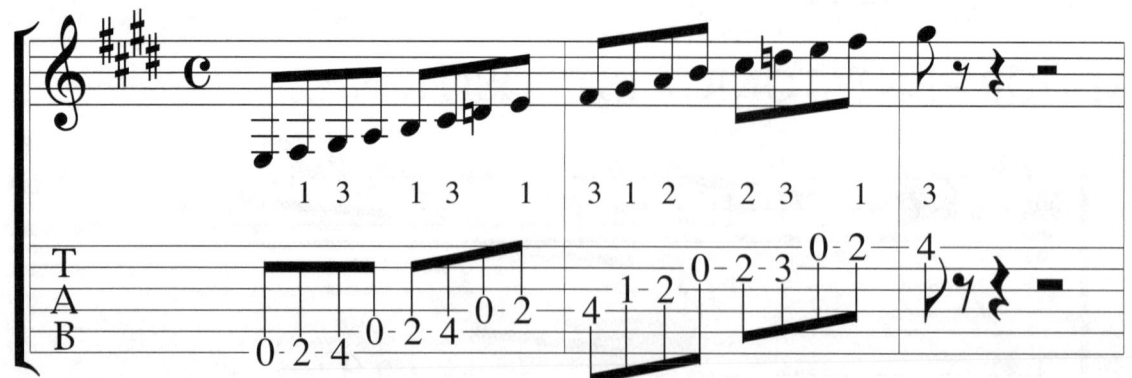

TIP!
There are devices to slow down the guitar licks on a CD without changing pitch. They are great for learning your favorite player's licks.

 **LICK 1**

This lick is simply a trill using the Em pentatonic scale. Make sure the pull offs are clean by playing on the tip of your finger.

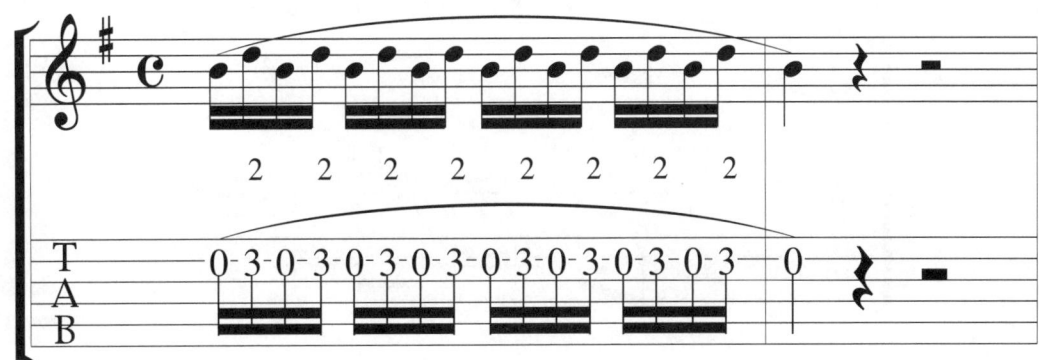

 **LICK 2**

Lick 2 is a mix of E minor and E major pentatonic.

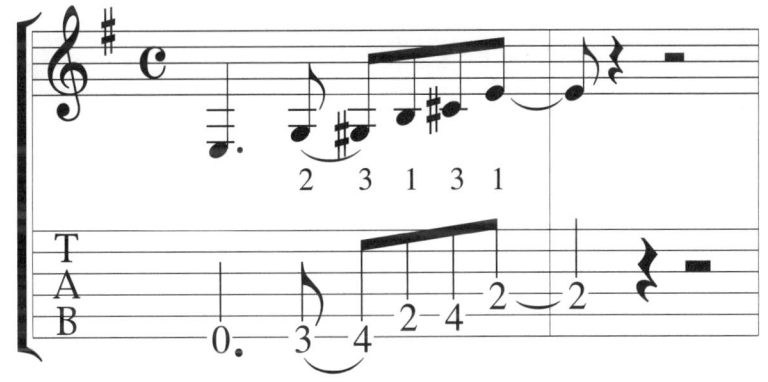

 **LICK 3**

This lick comes out of E Mixolydian which is an E major scale with a flat seventh. The pull offs should be clean and even. The slow version on the audio CD and DVD is played half as fast as written.

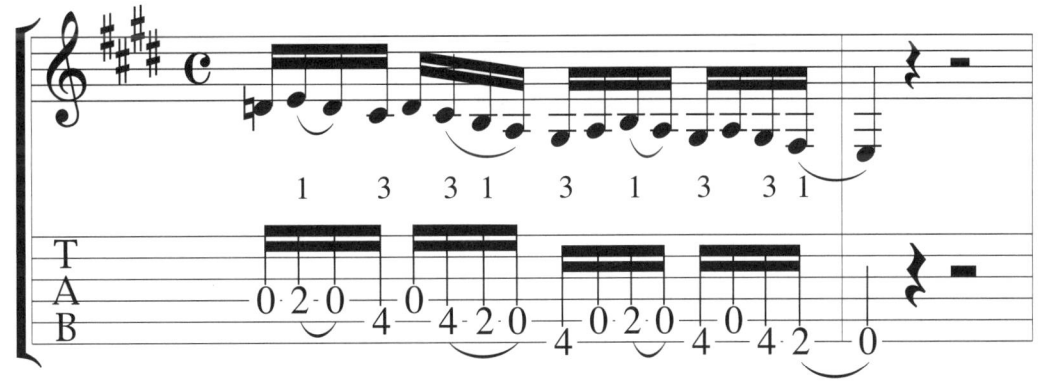

TIP!
Keep your guitar looking good with guitar polish. Never use furniture polish or cleaner.

 ## LICK 4

This lick comes out of the E major pentatonic scale 4th position. Make sure the bend gets up to pitch.

LICK 5

This lick starts with a double stop and a bend. It comes from the Em pentatonic scale 4th position.

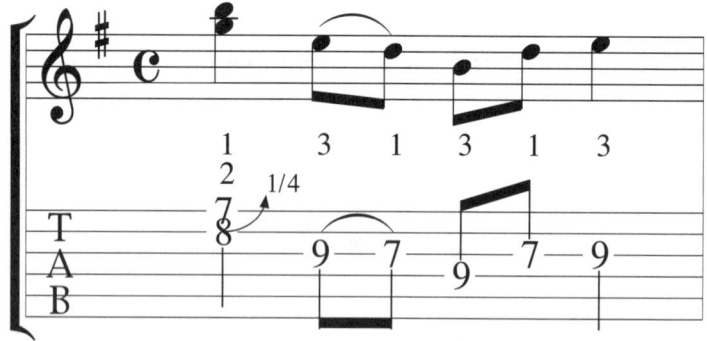

 ## THE EFFECTS OPTION

Try playing Lick 5 using a wah pedal. Listen to the CD or DVD to hear what this sounds like.

LICK 6

Here' a cool lick mixing Em and E major pentatonic.

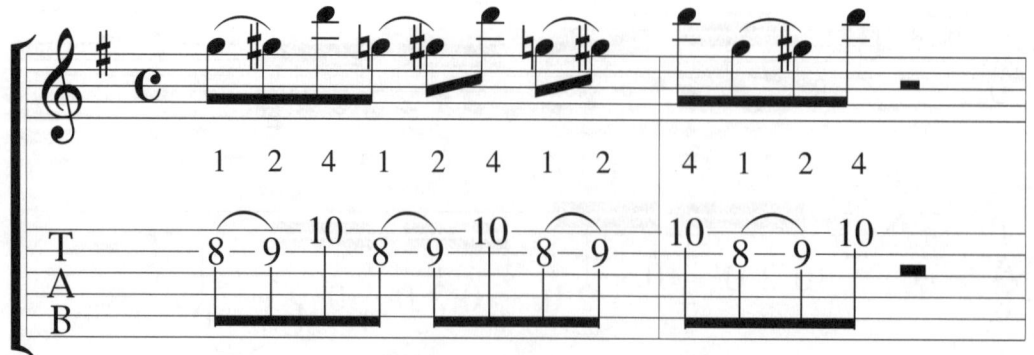

TIP!
Take a inexpensive recorder to your lessons so you can review each lesson later.

LICK 7

Here is a short lick out of the E minor pentatonic scale at the 12th fret. A very common lick.

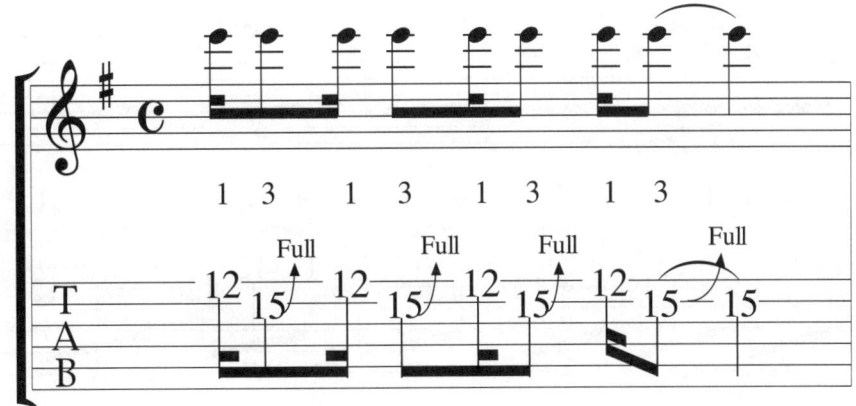

LICK 8

This lick is out of the Em pentatonic scale at the 12th fret and includes a tapped note using the right hand. Tapping is using a finger on your right hand to hammer on or pull off at a certain fret.

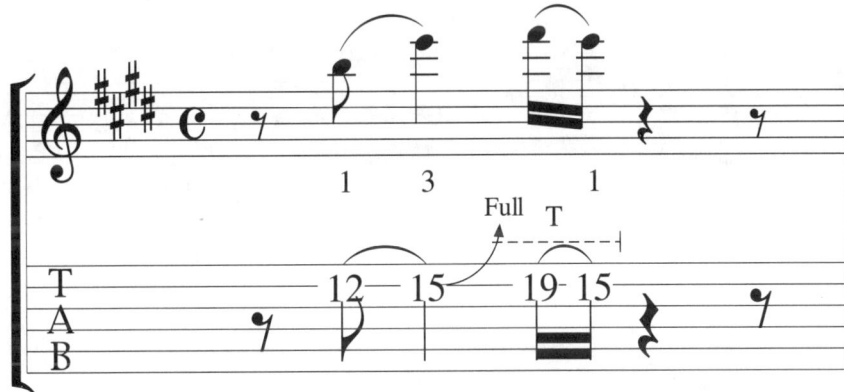

LICK 9

Lick 9 is a double stop lick. It sounds best using tremolo picking.

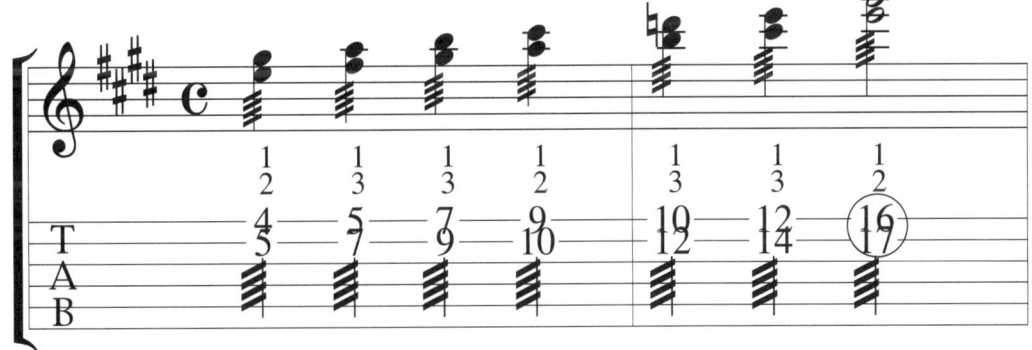

TIP!
Loosen the strings on your guitar when flying or going through the mountains. It will help prevent damage.

 ## LICK 10

Lick 10 is a E major lick. Keep the first and second string barred. It's all pull offs from there.

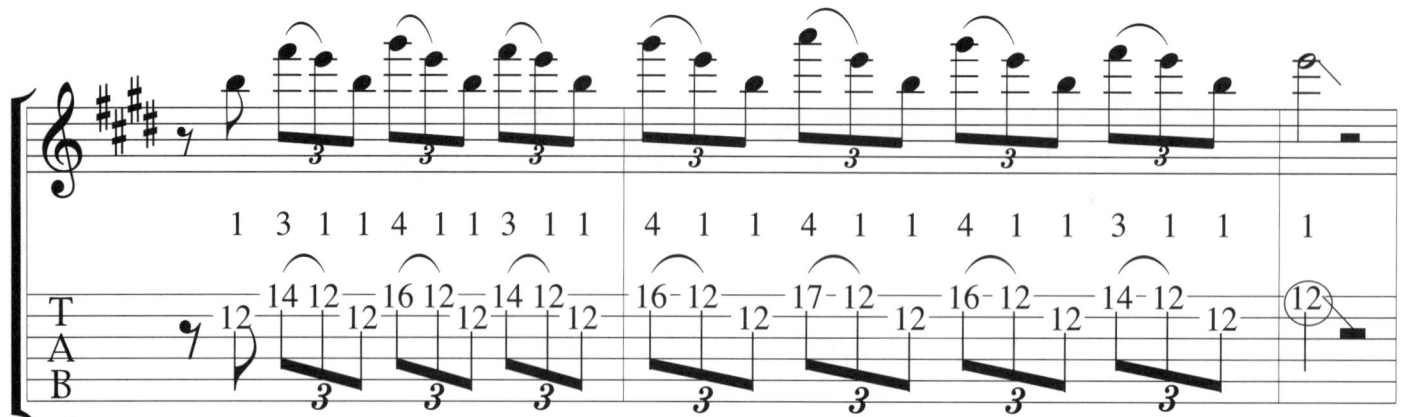

 ## LICK 11

This lick is from the Em blues scale 1st position. It also includes a major 3rd, G sharp.

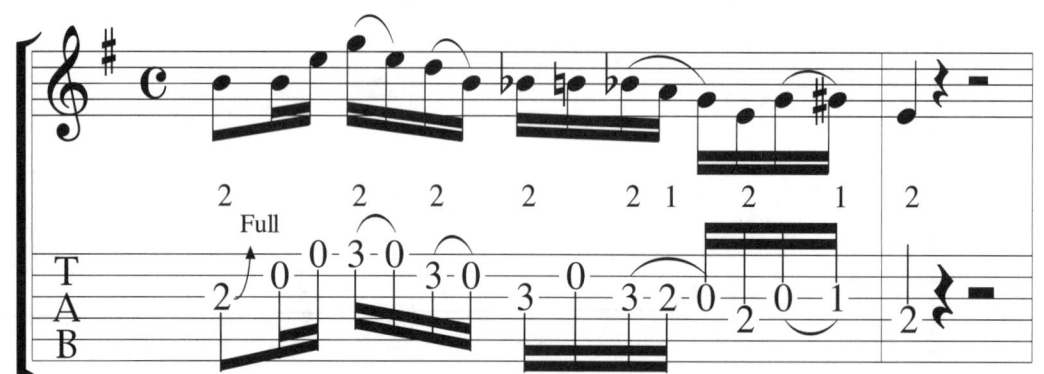

 ## LICK 12

This lick is out of the extended E major pentatonic scale.

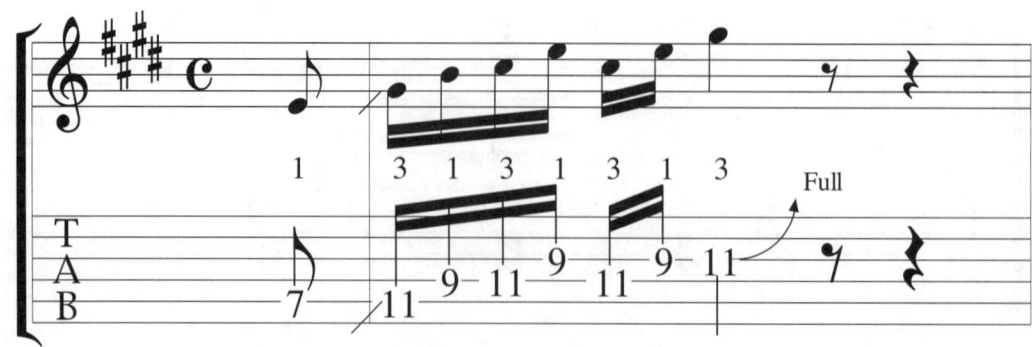

TIP!
Practice using a music stand. People tend to practice longer and more comfortably.

 ## LICK 13

Here is a lick out of the E major pentatonic scale at the 9th fret. It starts with a double hammer on.

 ## LICK 14

This is a common lick in E using the E Mixolydian scale.

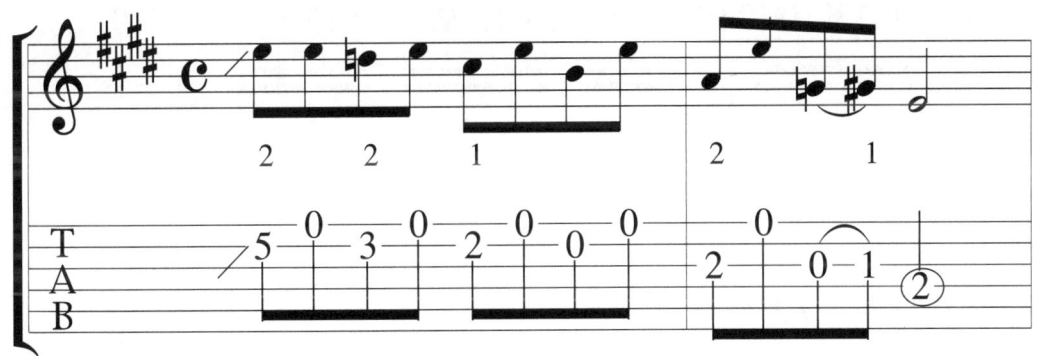

 ### THE EFFECTS OPTION

Try playing Lick 14 using a chorus pedal. Listen to the CD or DVD to hear what this sounds like.

TIP!
Practice licks at a relaxed speed and then move that relaxed feel slowly up the metronome.

 LICK 15

Here is a lick that starts with a trill and then moves down chromatically from Em pentatonic to E major pentatonic. Make sure the pull offs are crisp by playing on the tips of your fingers.

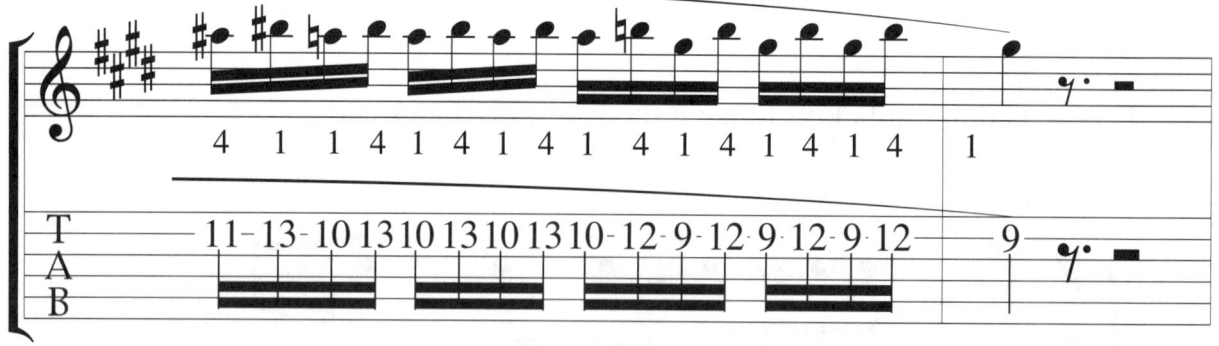

 THE EFFECTS OPTION

Try playing Lick 15 using a flanger pedal. Listen to the CD or DVD to hear what this sounds like.

TIP!
Using a peg winder will speed up the string changing process.

PRACTICING WITH THE LET'S JAM TRACK

    Included on the CD and DVD is a track with the licks played over Track 5 of the *Hard Rock Let's Jam! CD*. This is meant to give you an example of how these licks should sound. Listen to this track but don't necessarily try to play along with it. Once you are comfortable with several licks, try playing with the blank Let's Jam track provided with the CD (Track 96) or DVD (Special Features Section). This will give you a track to practice the same lick over and over. Try different phrasing and timings of the lick. Make it your own lick.

    On the next two pages is a listing of the 15 licks we have learned in this section. These are placed here to make it easy to work with the licks played along with the Let's Jam track. These licks are played in one group of 15 on the CD and three groups of five on the DVD. Notice the markers on the next two pages.

CD 74

PLAYING WITH TRACK 5 LET'S JAM! CD HARD ROCK

DVD VIDEO 5.44

Lick 1

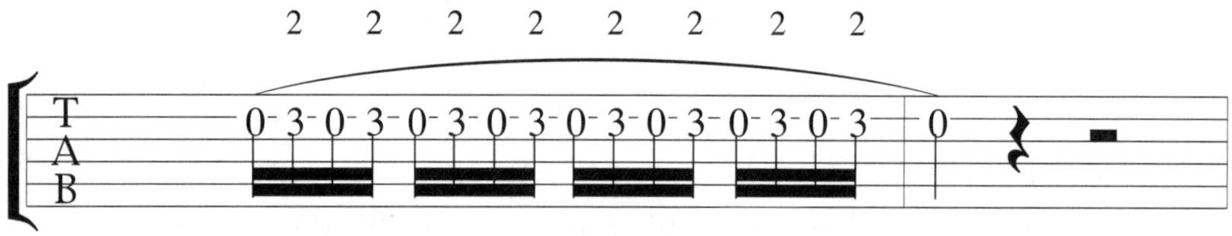

Lick 2

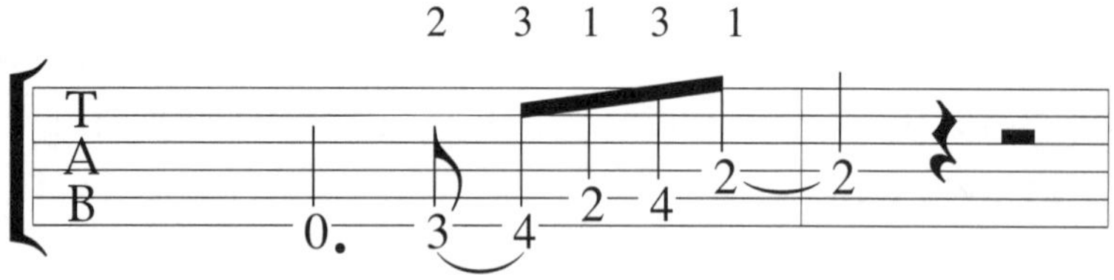

Lick 3

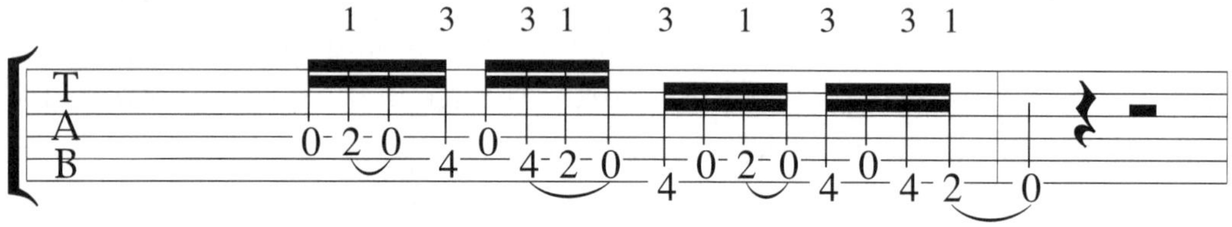

Lick 4

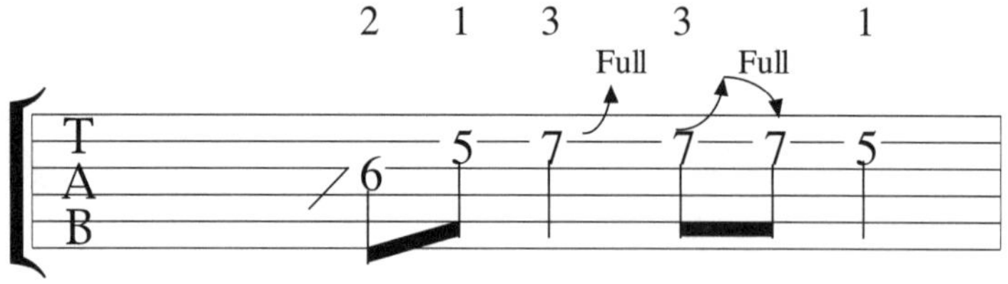

Lick 5

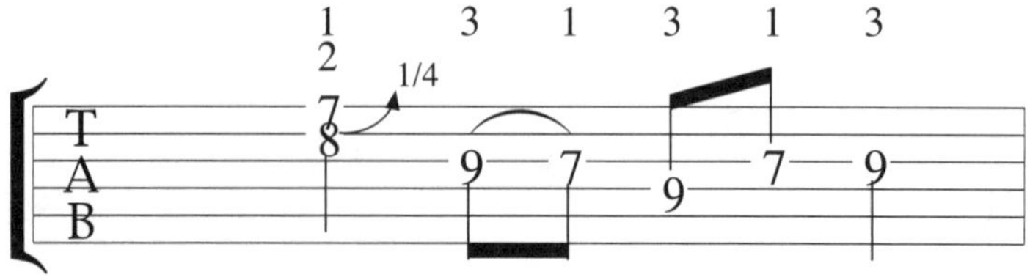

Lick 6

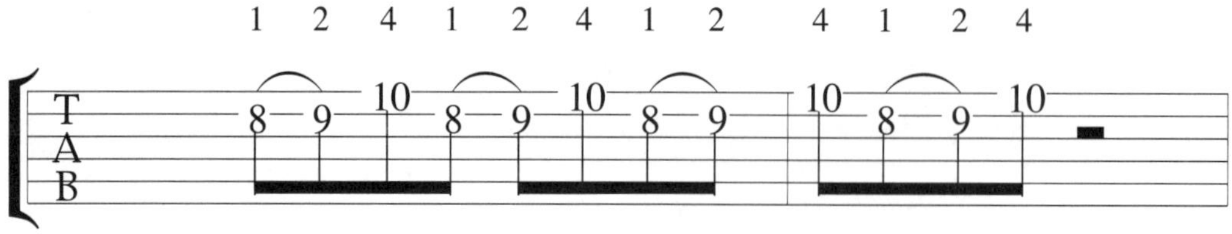

DVD VIDEO 5.45-5.46

Lick 7

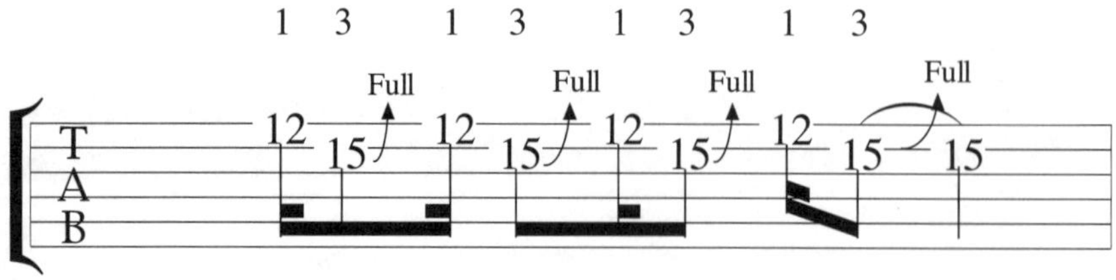

Lick 8

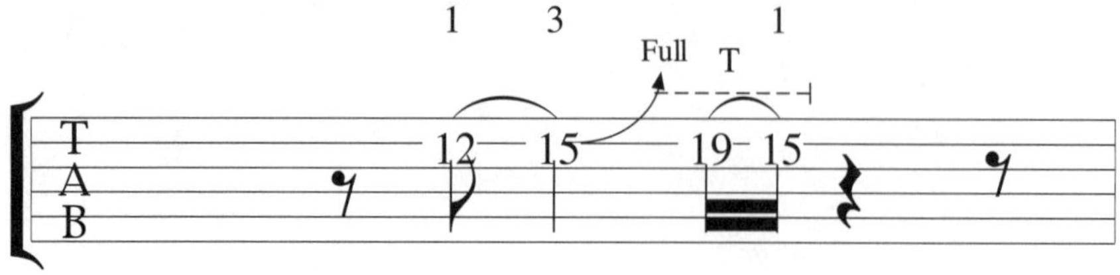

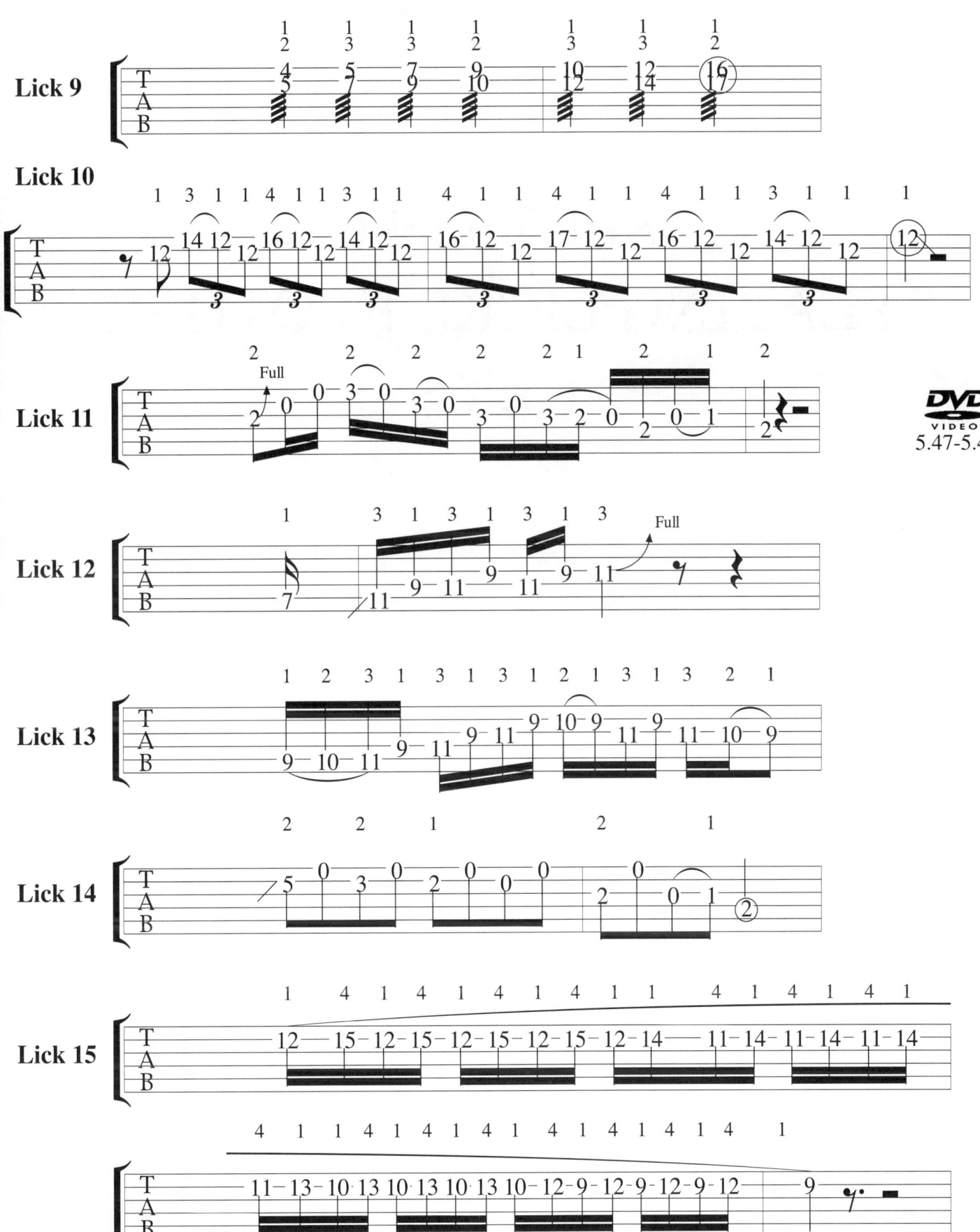

SECTION 6
PLAYING LICKS IN OTHER KEYS

Once you have mastered a lick, it is important to be able to play the same lick in other keys and along with other types of tunes. In this chapter, we will use examples of licks found previously in this book and transpose them to other keys and other feels. Use these examples to learn how to transpose licks yourself and then use this process with all the licks you have learned.

LICK 2 IN A MINOR - PAGE 14

This lick comes out of the first position of the Am pentatonic scale.

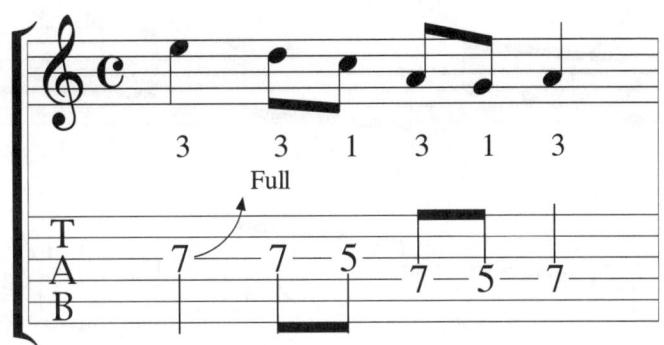

G MINOR PENTATONIC - 1ST POSITION

Let's play this lick in G minor. To do this, we will simply find the Gm pentatonic scale, which is at the 3rd fret or 2 frets lower than Am. Then play this lick using the notes in the Gm pentatonic scale.

LICK 2 IN G MINOR

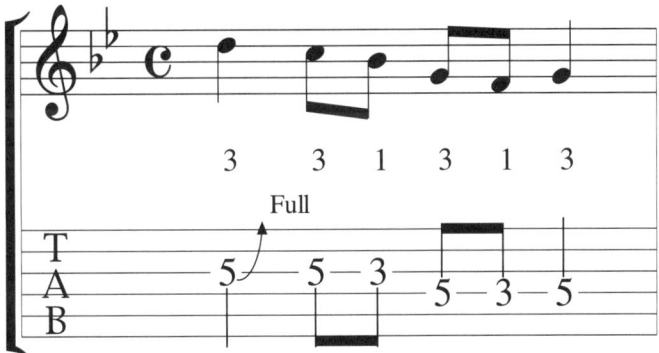

TIP!
If you learn music theory, you won't have to memorize as much. You will understand the logic of music.

LICK 2 IN E MINOR

Now let's learn this lick one more time, but this time in E minor. First find the Em pentatonic scale and then find the notes this lick uses within that scale. This lick actually sounds good over tunes in either E minor or E major.

E MINOR PENTATONIC - 12TH FRET

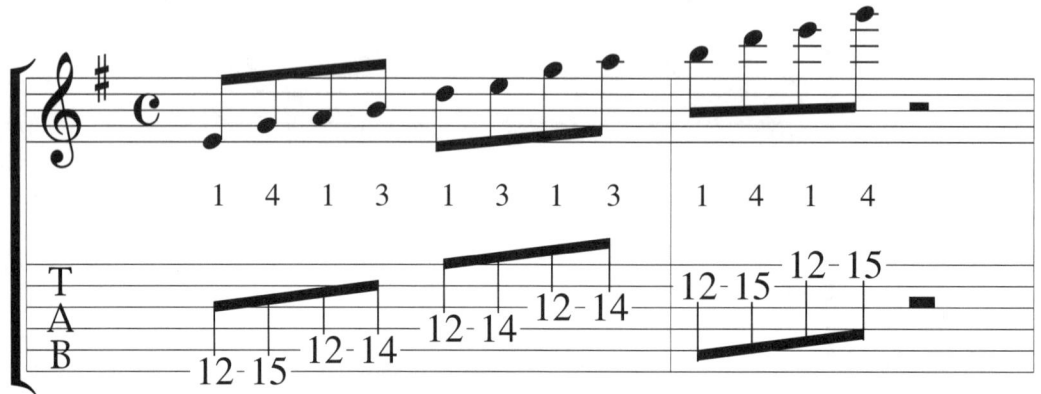

LICK 2 IN E MINOR

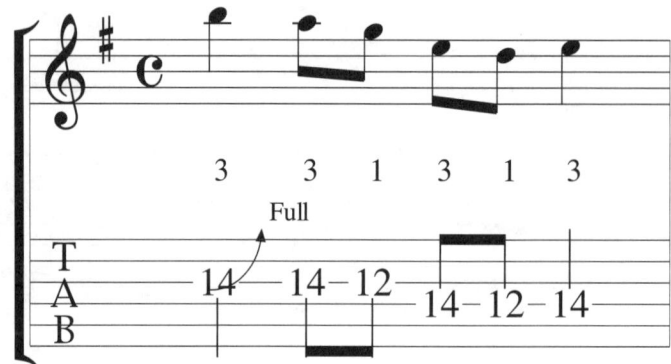

TIP!
Never believe anything you read in a fortune cookie.

LICK 1 IN A - PAGE 35

Let's try another lick, this time Lick 1 in A.

E BLUES WITH A MAJOR THIRD

We'll take this lick and learn to play it in E. First notice what notes from the A blues scale with a major third (page 33) this lick uses. Then look at the E blues scale with a major third and use this scale and these notes to play Lick 1 in E.

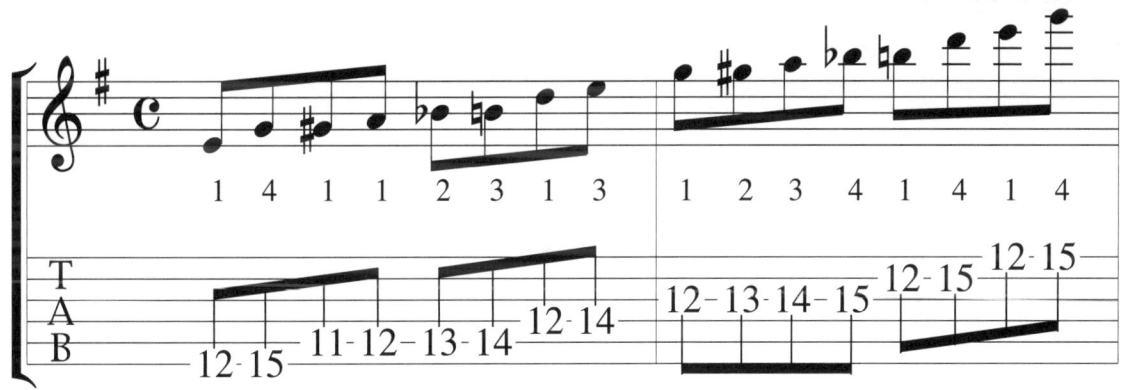

LICK 1 IN E

TIP!
Practice every day instead of trying to practice too much in one day.

LICK 1 IN G

Now take this same lick but play it in G minor. First practice the G blues scale with a major third.

 **G BLUES SCALE WITH MAJOR THIRD**

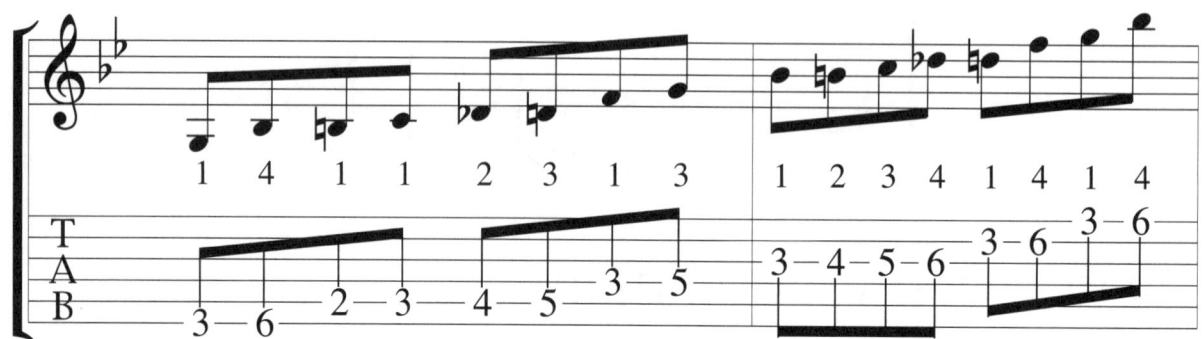

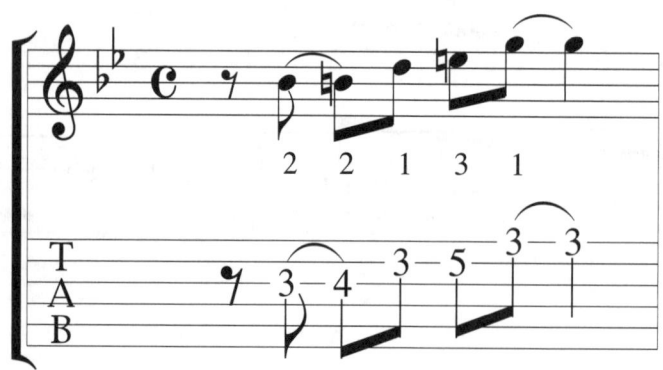

TIP!
Use a guitar cloth to clean your guitar and wipe it down after you play.

LICK 13 IN E - PAGE 49

6.14

This lick is out of the E major pentatonic scale.

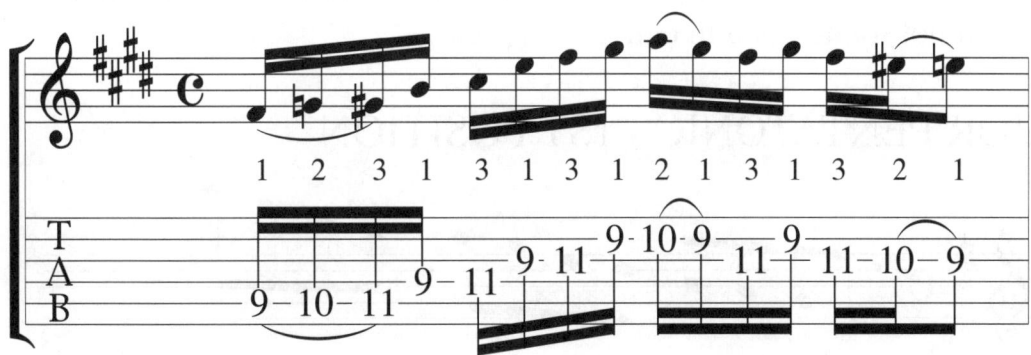

A MAJOR PENTATONIC - 1ST POSITION

6.15-6.16

We will transpose this lick into A major. See how this lick fits into the E major pentatonic scale and then use the same notes within the A major pentatonic scale.

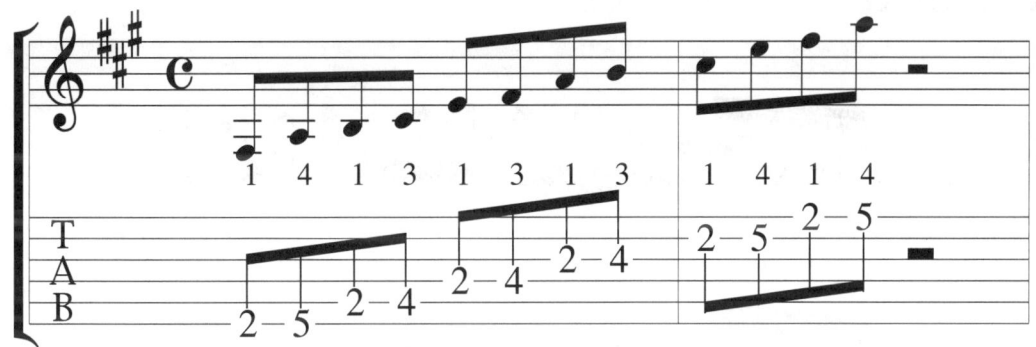

LICK 13 IN A

6.17

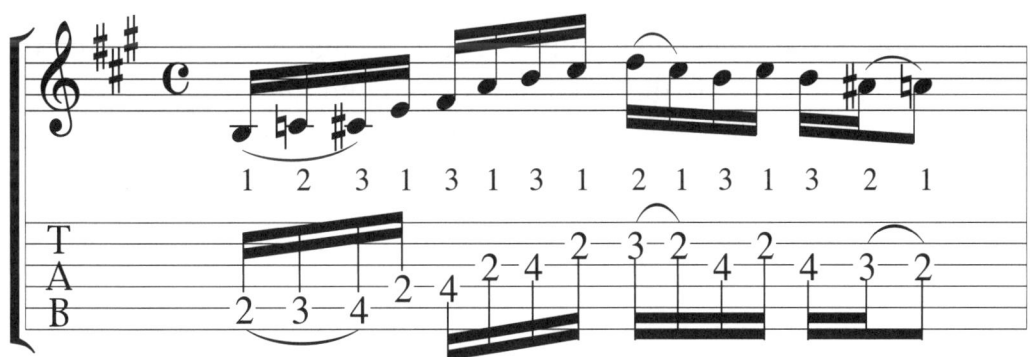

TIP!
Have your intonation checked by a professional.

LICK 9 IN G

Let's take the same lick and play it once again, but this time in G. Remember this is a lick based on the major pentatonic scale with a couple of extra notes added. This lick will not sound good in Gm.

 ## G MAJOR PENTATONIC - 1ST POSITION

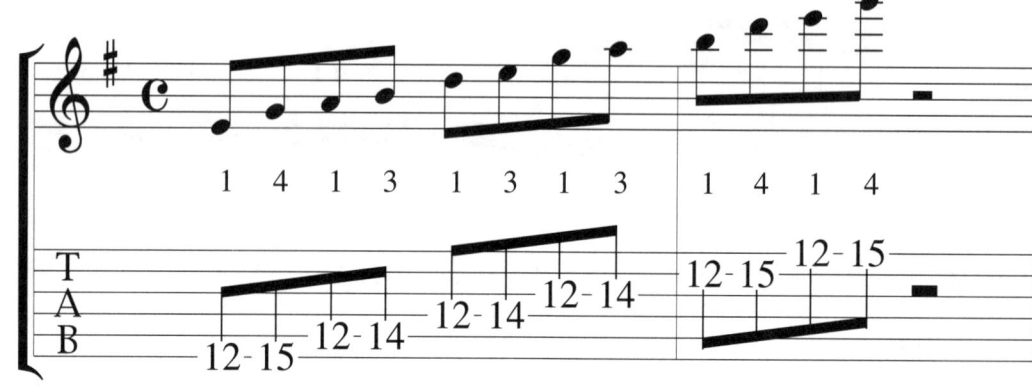

 ## LICK 13 IN G

TRANSPOSING OTHER LICKS

Now take any of the other licks you have learned and work on playing them in other keys. Look at what scale the lick comes from and then learn that scale in the new key. Take the same notes from that scale and play the lick in a new key. Practice this with as many licks in as many keys as possible.

TIP!

Typically, the lighter the wood, the brighter the sound of a guitar. Darker woods give darker tones.

SECTION 7
PRACTICING WITH LET'S JAM CDS

PRACTICING SCALES

One of the best ways to use the *Let's Jam CDs* is to simply practice the correct scale in rhythm with the audio. With *Let's Jam CDs*, each track comes with a suggestion of what scales to practice. These suggestions are found in the booklet that comes with the CD. For example, let's use track 4 on the *Let's Jam! CD Blues & Rock*. This track is also used in this book in our first section of licks and is included on the accompanying audio CD. We will use the 1st position Am pentatonic scale to practice over this tune.

A MINOR PENTATONIC - 1ST POSITION

Exercise 1

Try playing this scale in a slow rhythm. Play this scale forward and backwards using quarter notes. Try practicing using alternate picking.

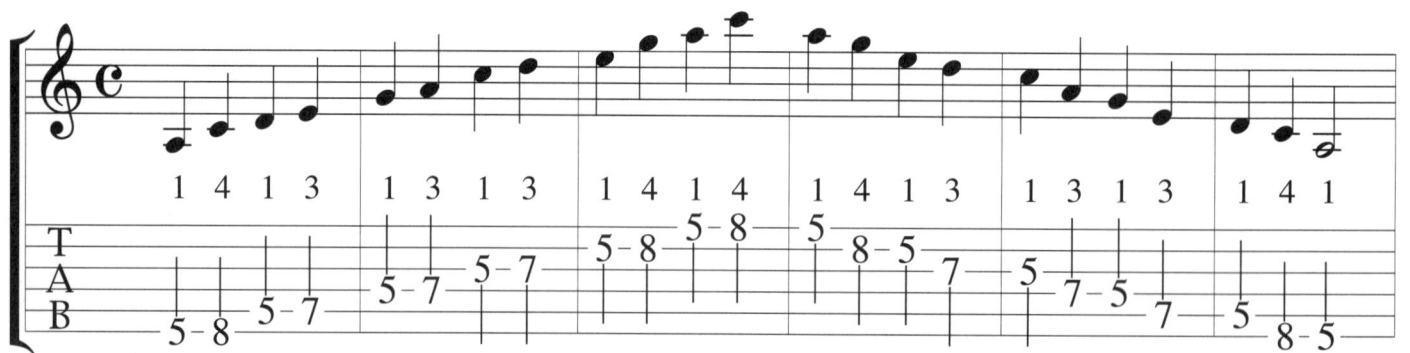

Exercise 2

Using the same scale, we'll now play 8th notes. This will be twice as fast as before. Once again, use alternate picking and play the scale forwards and backwards.

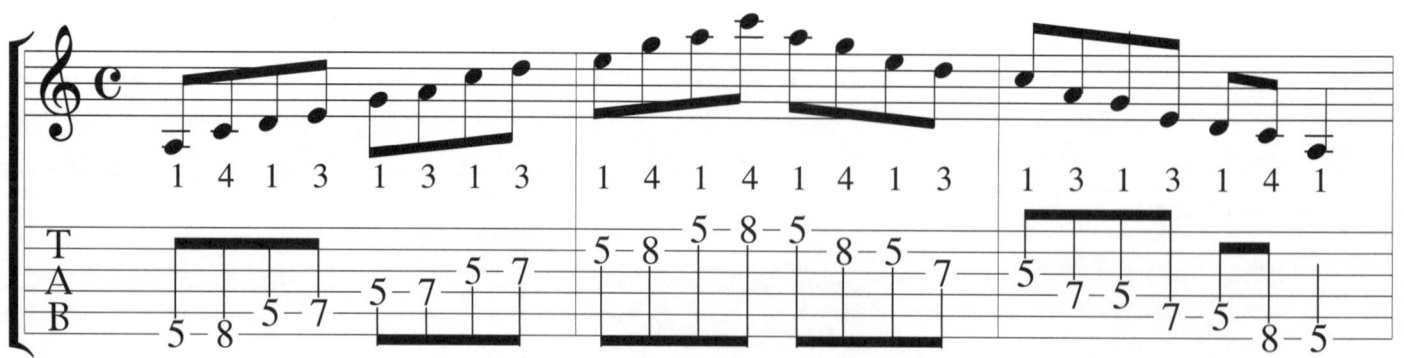

TIP!
Have strap locks installed on your guitar. It will help keep your guitar from falling.

Exercise 3

Now play the same scale again using 16th notes. Use alternate picking and play the scale forward and backwards.

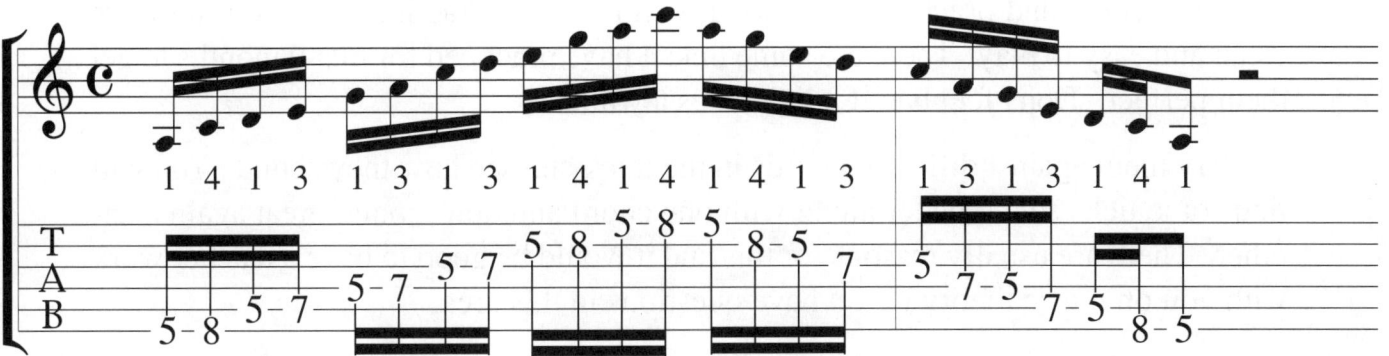

Exercise 4

Another great way to practice is to mix up the scale so you play it different every time. Be spontaneous with this practice but try to be logical as well. Keep your playing as continuous as possible. Listen to the audio CD and then try it yourself.

Use these techniques with all the positions of whatever scale you are using. For more information on scales and their positions, try *The Guitarist's Scale Book*. Try this practice technique with all the tracks on a Let's Jam CD and you will become proficient in many keys.

TIP!
When finishing a gig, pack up your guitars first. It prevents damage.

PRACTICING LICKS WITH LET'S JAM CD

Now that you have a vast array of licks at your disposal, let's look at ways to work with these licks with the *Let's Jam CDs*. First, it is most important to learn the licks as written and practice them along with the CD. Practice them until they are clean and easy to play. There are some licks I have practiced for many months to get them perfect. Don't feel bad if a lick takes a while.

Try them against different chords in the track and see how they sound. You will find some licks sound better along with one chord and don't sound great against another. There are usually reasons for this and it would be good to have a teacher work with you on music theory if you have questions in this area.

Second, practice starting them at different times. Try starting them on downbeats and upbeats. Try starting them on the & of 4 or the & of 1. This will change the sound and feel of the lick dramatically. This concept was discussed earlier in the Licks & Phrasing section on page 10. You can listen to the audio examples of that section to refresh your memory.

Practice each lick in different keys as discussed in the Playing Licks in Other Keys chapter. There are many different keys on each *Let's Jam CD*, so try your favorite licks against each track. You will learn how they sound in different keys and different feels as well.

Try making the licks your own by changing them slightly. Do this only after you have learned them as written. A different way of phrasing them and a different starting point both make the lick more your own and not simply quoting another guitar player.

Remember to not simply string licks together one after the other. Try burying the lick within a line as discussed on page 9. Use a sequence of notes before and after the lick to conceal that it is a lick. Make it hard to find. Listen to the audio examples from page 9 to refresh your memory on this concept.

Licks are great tools and a lot of fun to play. They are not the end goal however. Remember when using licks to solo, our goal is to create a melody. Hopefully an interesting melody that people will want to listen to. So practice those licks and use the *Let's Jam CDs* to help you. They are a valuable resource to become a better guitar player.

TIP!
Never practice electric guitar barefoot in the basement.

TAKE THE LET'S JAM CD TO LESSONS

Teachers can help you practice many more techniques and ideas along with these CDs. You can learn how to play the chords, more complicated rhythms, or how to practice with arpeggios. The CDs were designed to help you explore different styles of guitar playing. For example, the *Let's Jam! CD Blues & Rock* is great for practicing licks and pentatonic scales. The *Let's Jam! CD Jazz & Blues* is great for working on diatonic scales, modes, and 2-5-1 licks. The *Let's Jam! CD Hard Rock* is great for more aggressive use of distortion and rock licks. It also mixes up use of pentatonic scales, diatonic scales, and modes. Your teacher can help you explore these concepts. Your guitar teacher can also explain the theory behind the chords and the licks. This is invaluable to your continued growth as a guitar player.

TIP!
Experiment with different styles of guitar playing. You never know where your next breakthrough moment will come.

TWO SOLOS USING LICKS

Note - This section is a Bonus Section and is not included on the DVD. There are video clips of this section on our website: http://www.cvls.com/licks.html.

SOLO IN E MAJOR AND A MINOR

On the next two pages you will find two solos. The first solo is designed to use the licks in Section 5 and the second solo uses the licks in Section 2. Each solo is designed to demonstrate as many licks as possible. In actuality, one should not use so many licks in such a short period of time. It serves it's purpose here, however.

SOLO 1

This solo is over track 5 of the *Let's Jam! CD Hard Rock*. The licks are from Section 5. Here are the licks that are used:

1. Lick 3 starting in measure 1
2. Lick 4 starting in measure 3
3. Lick 5 starting in measure 5
4. Lick 12 starting in measure 7
5. Lick 7 starting in measure 9
6. Lick 14 starting in measure 13

SOLO 2

This solo is over track 4 of the *Let's Jam! CD Blues & Rock*. The licks are from Section 2. Here are the licks that are used:

1. Lick 1 starting in measure 1
2. Lick 9 starting in measure 2
3. Lick 7 starting in measure 4
4. Lick 3 starting in measure 5
5. Lick 10 starting in measure 7
6. Lick 4 starting in measure 9

Practice these solos slowly at first and then try to play along with the CD.

SOLO 1

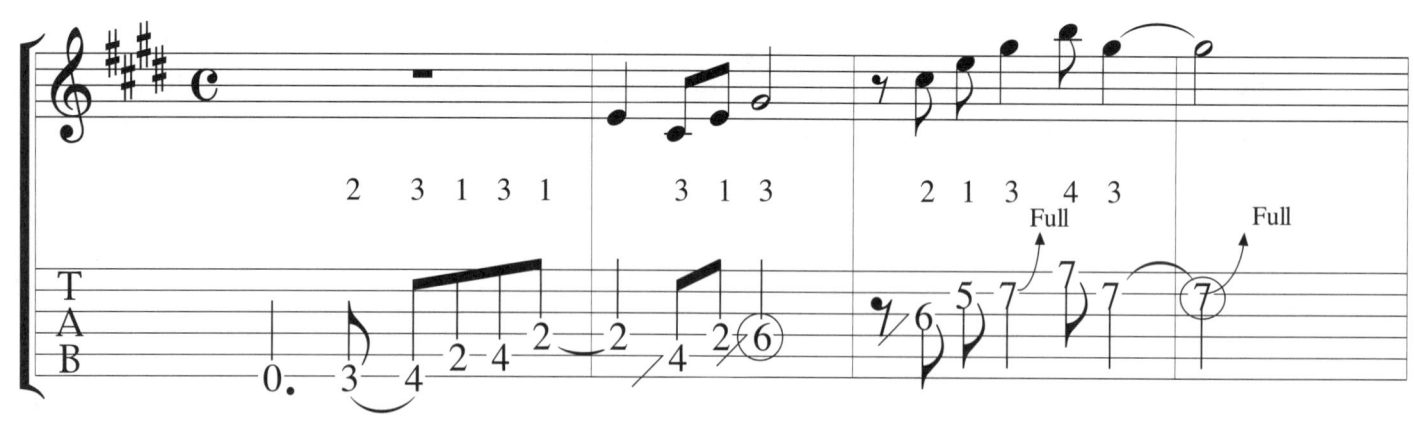

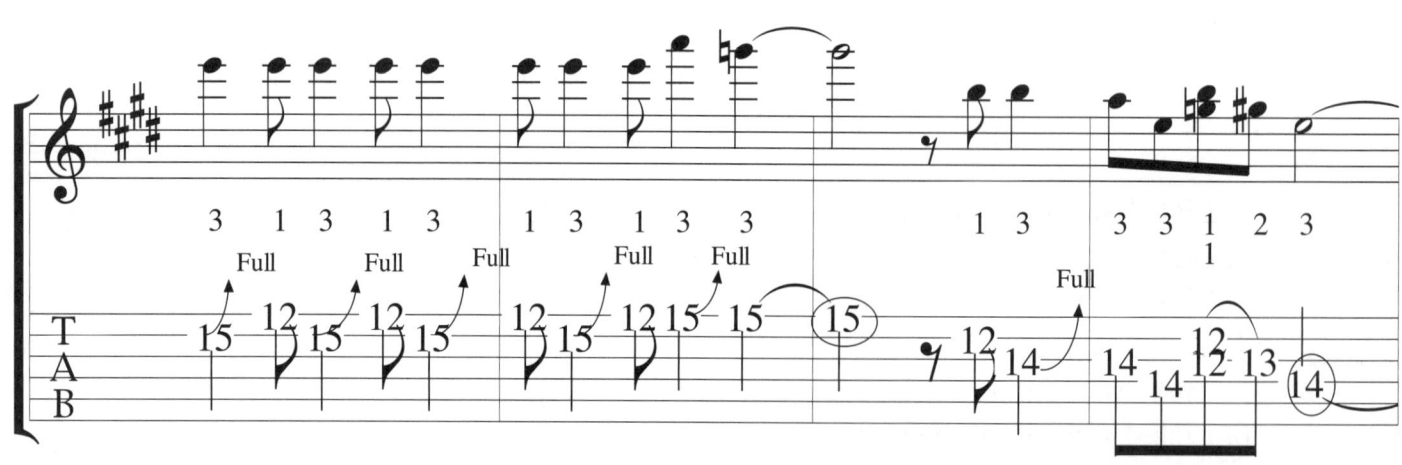
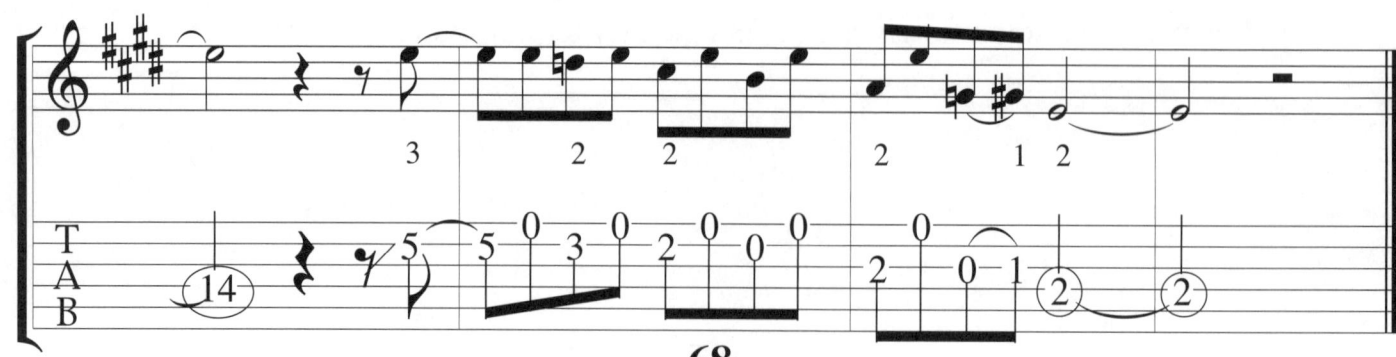

SOLO 2

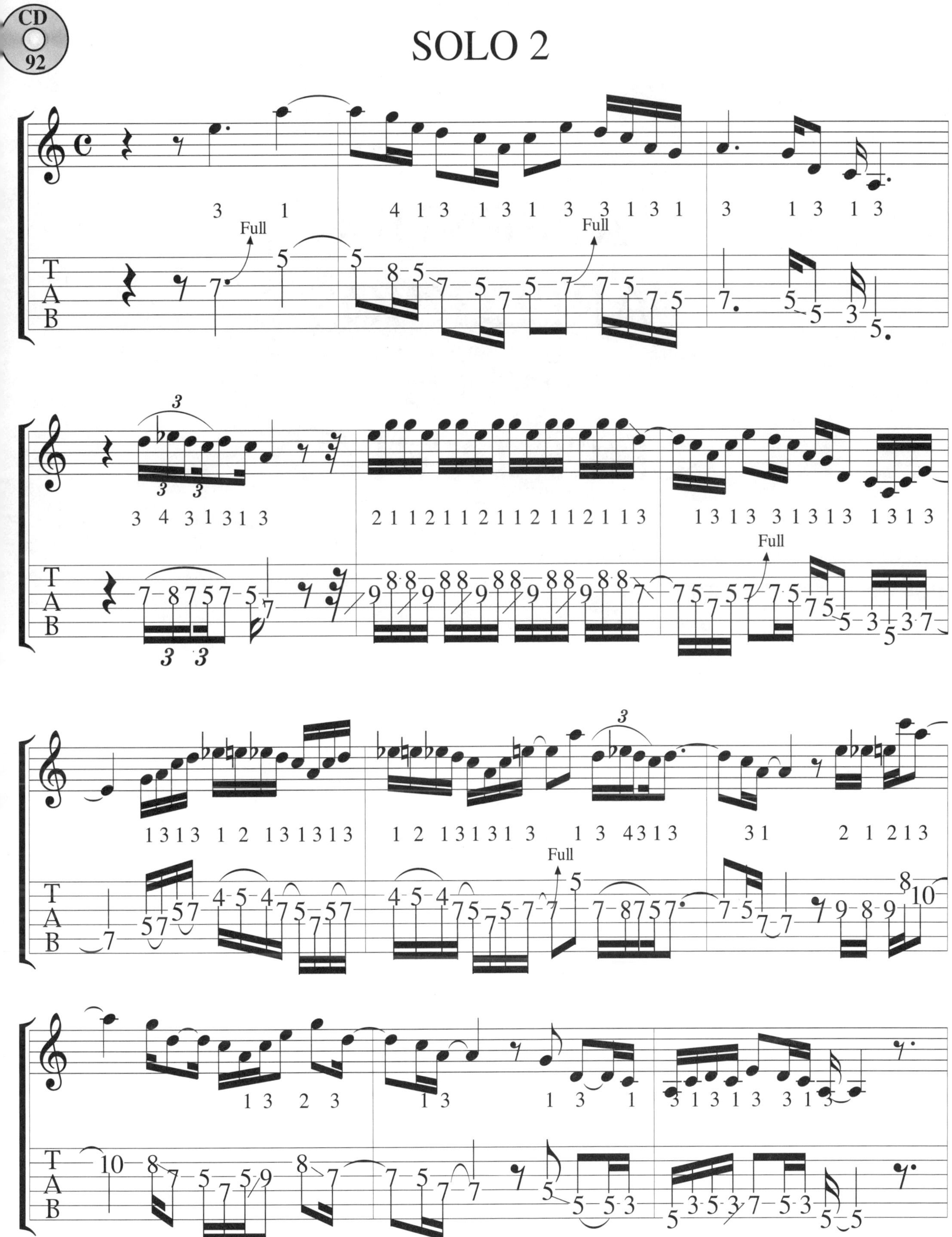

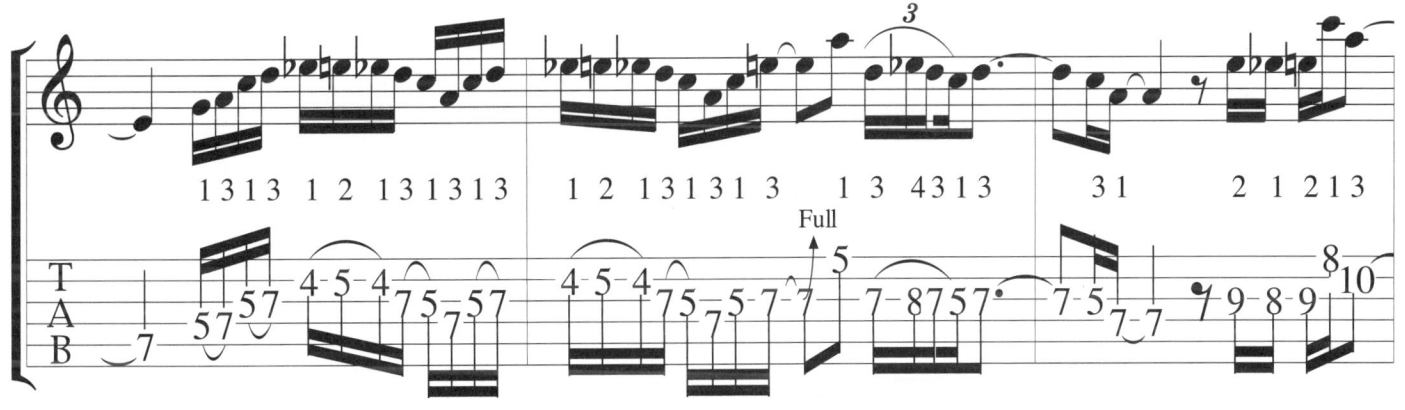

APPENDIX
ARPEGGIOS
WITH
LET'S JAM! CD

Note - This section is a Bonus Section and is not included on the CD or DVD. There are video clips on our website: http://www.cvls.com/licks.html.

ARPEGGIOS IN A MINOR

In this section, we will learn some useful arpeggio shapes to use along with track 4 of the *Let's Jam! CD Blues & Rock*. This track is in A minor and we will focus on arpeggios in that key. When improvising, players tend to use a combination of scales, arpeggios, and licks. An arpeggio is playing one note of a chord at a time. In this case we will use arpeggios that are useful to soloing applications. On this page are Am7 and Em7 arpeggios. Both sound great in Am.

A MINOR 7

E MINOR 7

A MINOR 7

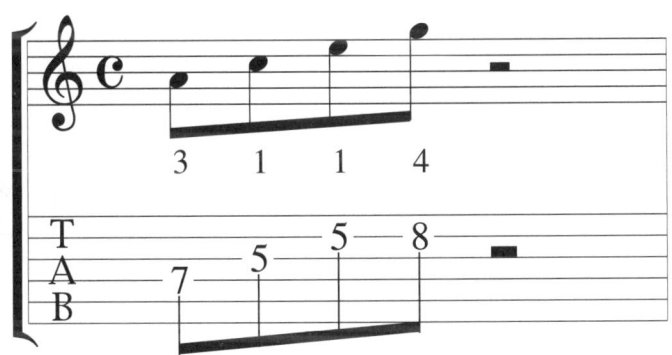

E MINOR 7

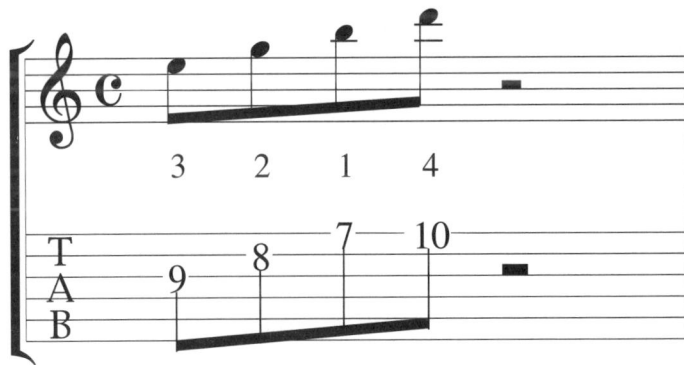

A MINOR 7

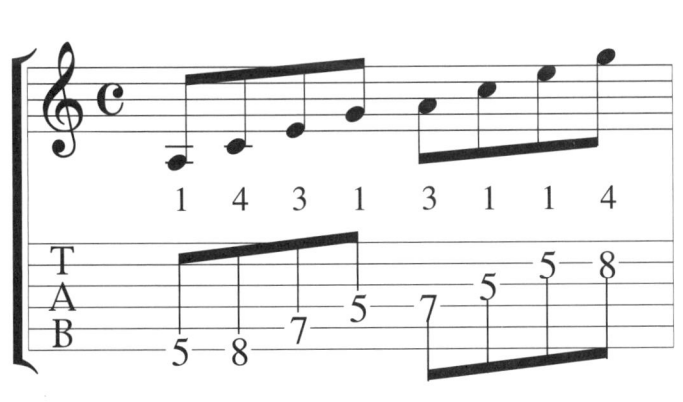

A MINOR 7

ARPEGGIOS IN G MINOR

Next we will learn arpeggio shapes to use along with track 15 of the *Let's Jam! CD Hard Rock*. This track is in G minor with a Dorian feel or sound. This means the sixth degree of the scale, in this case the note Eb, is raised a half step to E. To understand this more, you may wish to purchase the *Guitarist's Scale Book,* which has a great explanation of the modes. We have Gm7, Dm7, and FM7 arpeggios in this section. FM7 has the E natural or Dorian note.

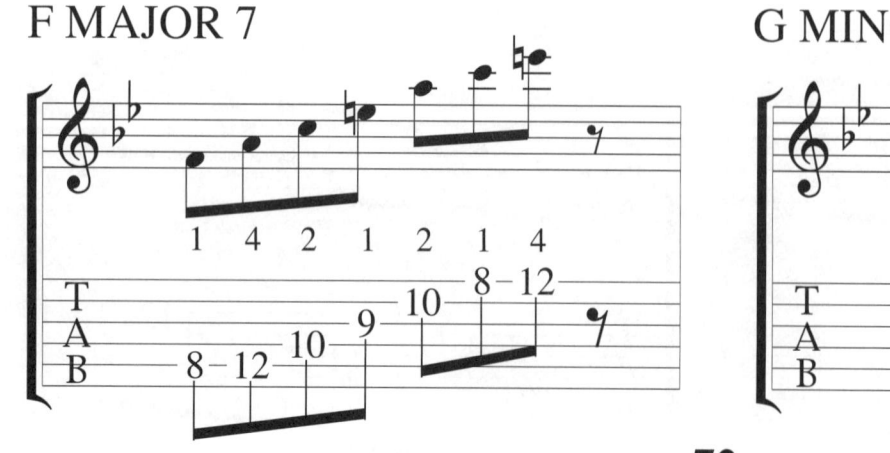

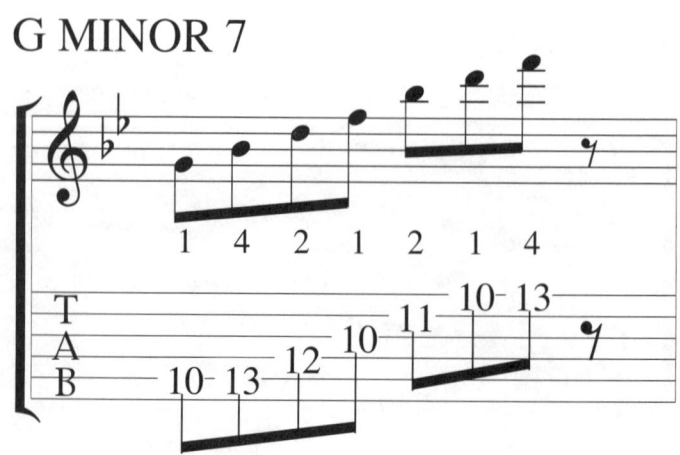

ARPEGGIOS IN A

In this section we will learn arpeggio shapes to use along with track 4 of the *Let's Jam! CD Jazz & Blues*. This track is in A with a strong blues flavor. Our arpeggios will reflect this sound and all of them for this example are A7 arpeggios. Learn the arpeggios forward and backwards and then play the notes in any order. Be creative.

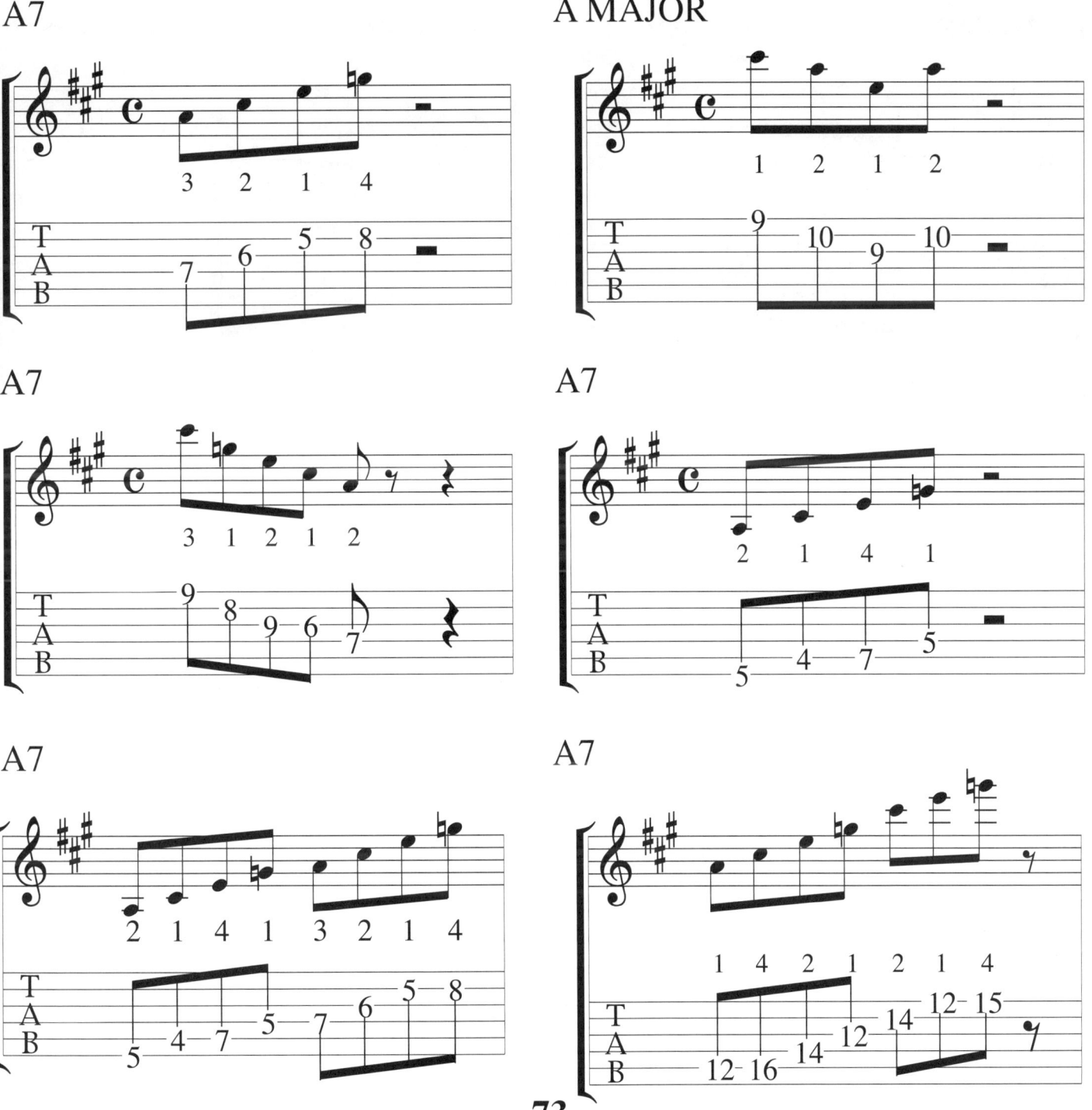

ARPEGGIOS IN E MAJOR

In this section we will learn arpeggio shapes to use along with track 5 of the *Let's Jam! CD Hard Rock*. This track is in E major with a heavy rock sound. The arpeggios we choose to use and how we play them should reflect this sound. We have E major and C#m7 arpeggios on this page. When you are proficient with an arpeggio, try to use the arpeggio within a melody or solo line. Use an arpeggio as you would use any scale or lick.

E MAJOR

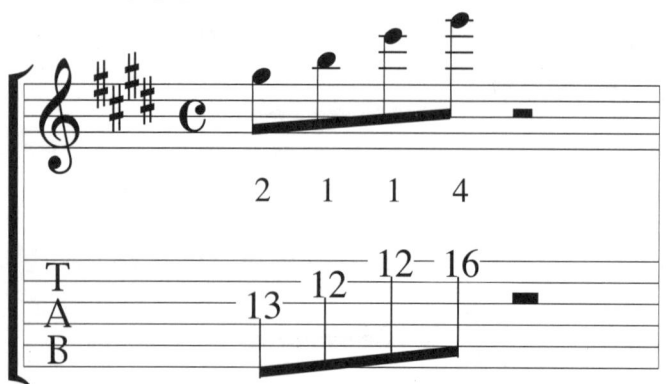

E MAJOR

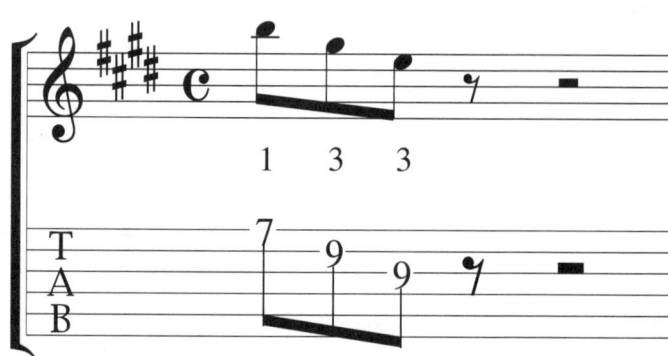

E MAJOR

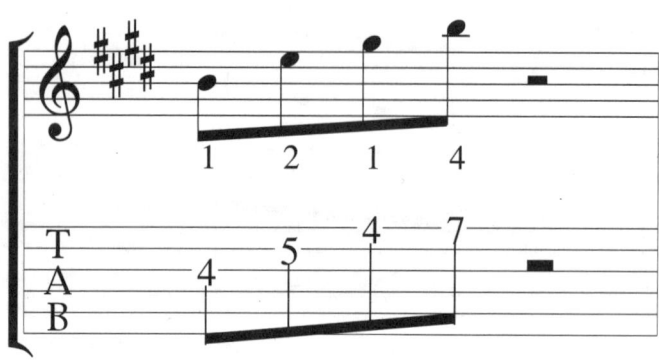

C# MINOR 7

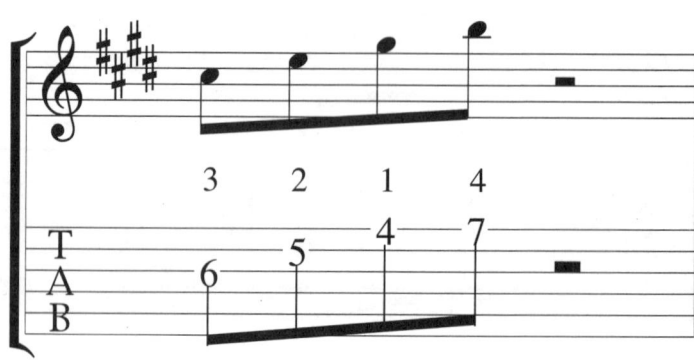

E MAJOR

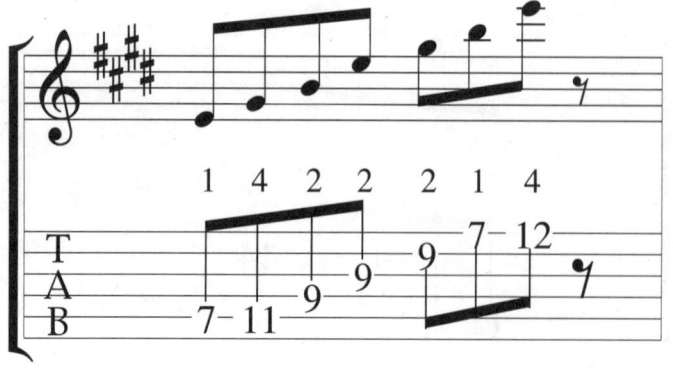

C# MINOR 7

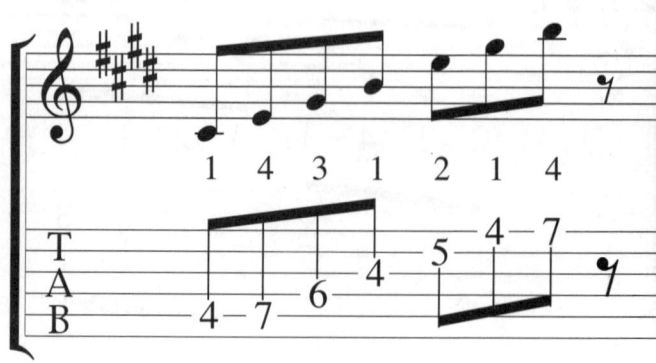